DARK ELVES

A WARHAMMER ARMIES SUPPLEMENT

CONTENTS

Written by
Gav Thorpe, Space James McQuirk and
Tuomas Pirinen

Illustrations and Graphics
David Gallagher

Cover Illustration
Geoff Taylor

Map drawn by
Nuala Kennedy

Colour Production
Adrian Wood

Editing and Layout
Mark Owen

Citadel Designers
Dave Andrews, Mark Bedford, Juan Diaz,
Chris Fitzpatrick, Alex Hedström,
Mark Harrison, Gary Morley,
Aly Morrison and Trish Morrison

Model Makers
Mark Jones and Dave Andrews

Miniatures Painters
Martin Footitt, Neil Green,
Tammy Haye, Kirsten Mickleburgh,
Keith Robertson, Chris Smart,
and Dave Thomas

Thanks also to
Alessio Cavatore, Jake Thorton,
Rick Priestley, Gordon Davidson,
Matt Sulley, Gareth Harvey and
Erik 'Poom' Mogensen

PRODUCED BY GAMES WORKSHOP

UK	**US**	**Australia**	**Canada**
Games Workshop,	Games Workshop,	Games Workshop,	2679 Bristol Circle,
Willow Rd,	6721 Baymeadow Drive,	23 Liverpool Street,	Units 2&3,
Lenton,	Glen Burnie,	Ingleburn	Oakville,
Nottingham, NG7 2WS	Maryland, 21060-6401	NSW 2565	Ontario, L6H 6Z8

Product Code: 60 03 02 12 001   Games Workshop World Wide Web site: www.games-workshop.com   **ISBN: 1-84154-083-8**

INTRODUCTION

Listen, young lord, and heed me well. I have been bidden to instruct you in the Art of War. We Druchii are the greatest exponents of warfare, and you must study hard that so you will not bring shame to the land of Naggaroth, your city, your house and ultimately your lord and master King Malekith.

You must learn to be cunning, for the slow-witted will be defeated by clever tacticians. You must be ruthless, for the honour-bound will lose the battle before it starts. But above all you must learn to be merciless, for we cannot allow weaklings to thrive while traitors still hold our ancestral lands. Thus I will instruct you, as is the command of Malekith, rightful Lord of Ulthuan, and one day you too may march your army upon the shores of our homeland.

Hear, my lord, of the Druchii. From distant Cathay to the usurped lands of our accursed kin, from the cold lands of Norsca to the steaming jungles of the Southlands, our armies are rightfully feared. We alone keep alive the great and noble traditions of our ancestors of Nagarythe. Only we follow the path laid by mighty Aenarion the Defender. Only we follow the True Way.

As it was in the ancient times, the glorious armies of the Witch King are drawn from the garrisons of our cities, bolstered by the elite formations such as the Executioners of Har Ganeth, and the mighty Cold One Knights. To become a commander who is feared by his enemies, you must learn the strengths and capabilities of your troops by heart. Heed me well as I recite the warriors that make up the Hosts of Naggaroth.

For an expert player there are few armies as rewarding to play as the Dark Elves. They are an army of hidden strengths and subtle power. Whereas a Chaos or Orc army might send all their troops forward in a mindless attack, and a cowardly Wood Elf army hangs back and shoots at their opponents, Dark Elves excel in all aspects of warfare.

The Dark Elf army has numerous specialised troops as well as many elite regiments. All Dark Elves are extremely skilled at using their weapons. They are fast moving and have good morale – all the hallmarks of a classic elite force.

Dark Elves can be played in many ways. Dark Elf Spearmen and Crossbowmen backed by the dreaded Reaper Bolt Throwers can be made into a fearsome defensive force, but many Dark Elf players prefer using the Druchii aggressively.

A well-led Dark Elf army on the offensive is a frightening opponent. Frenzied Witch Elves are more than a match for any enemy infantry, while the charge of the Cold One Knights can shatter even the most determined enemy lines. So the typical Dark Elf army is fast, very well equipped and extremely skilled in both mêlée and shooting.

Dark Elves have their weaknesses too. They are neither very tough, nor do they possess the high strength which some other races enjoy. They are also rather limited in their choice of war machines. The other thing to remember is that the Dark Elves are expensive in terms of points, which means your army must be very compact, and every regiment must fulfil their role. While the Skaven or Goblin player may ignore the loss of a regiment or two, a Dark Elf commander can ill afford such losses. It is the great tacticians who excel with the Dark Elves.

Warhammer Armies: Dark Elves breaks down into the four main sections listed below, each of which illuminates a different area of creating your own Dark Elf force and getting it into action on the battlefield.

The Dark Host. Describes the unique troops, creatures and war machines of the Dark Elf army and gives full details of their rules.

The Army List. This provides all of the points values, weapon options and upgrades for you to field a Dark Elf army in games of Warhammer.

Painting and Collecting Guide. This section shows examples of Dark Elf colour schemes and markings, gives advice on choosing your own schemes, and tips on painting and modelling.

The Land of Chill. The back of this book is dedicated to extra information revealing the character, history and heroes of the Dark Elves and their bleak land of Naggaroth.

The Elven Kingdoms

Far across the Great Ocean to the west of the Old World lies the vast continent of Naggaroth. It is a harsh and rugged wilderness above which dark clouds gather to unleash terrible storms upon the land. Beneath the massive mountain ranges lie a huge network of underground caverns through which the Dark Elves sail their dread Black Arks to launch surprise raids on the distant kingdoms of the Old World and further afield to Nippon and Cathay. But the principle target for Dark Elf invasion is the magical isle of Ulthuan, the majestic homeland of all Elven kind, from which this Dark Kindred were exiled many millenia ago.

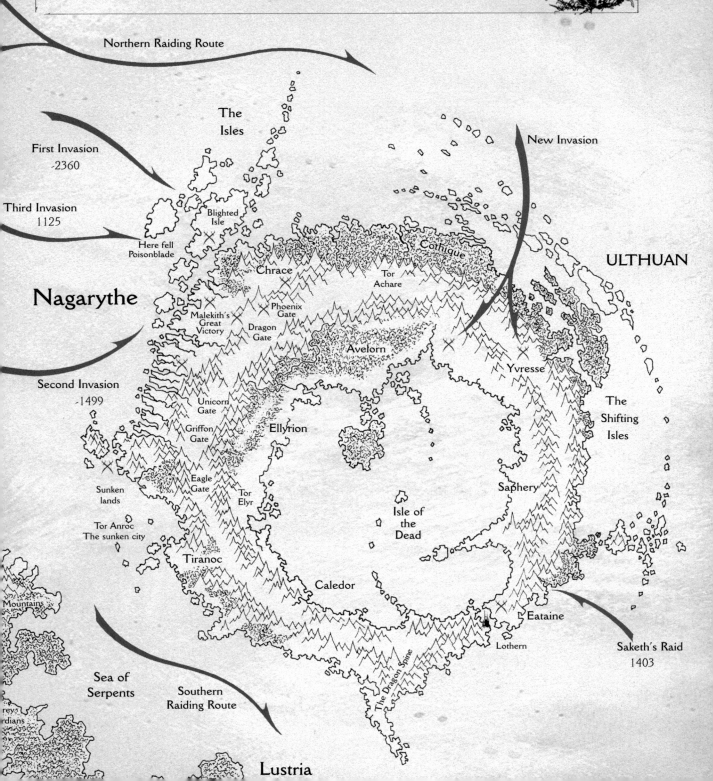

Northern Raiding Route

The Isles

First Invasion
-2360

Third Invasion
1125

Here fell
Poisonblade

Blighted
Isle

Chrace

Cothique

Tor
Achare

Nagarythe

Malekith's
Great
Victory

Phoenix
Gate

Dragon
Gate

Avelorn

New Invasion

ULTHUAN

Yvresse

Second Invasion
-1499

Unicorn
Gate

Griffon
Gate

Ellyrion

The
Shifting
Isles

Saphery

Eagle
Gate

Tor
Elyr

Isle of
the
Dead

Sunken
lands

Tor Anroc
The sunken city

Tiranoc

Caledor

Eataine

Lothern

Saketh's Raid
1403

Mountains

Sea of
Serpents

Southern
Raiding Route

The Dragon Spine

reys
dians

Lustria

THE DARK HOST

Many and varied are the highly skilled warriors of the Witch King. Master the arts of strategy and tactics so that you might better settle the bitter debt owed by the fallen Kin of Ulthuan. Unleash the fury of the Druchii upon your foes and be glad that you do Khaine's great work.

DARK ELF WARRIORS

Much of your army is raised from the population of our cities. Amongst our ranks march our wives and sisters: beautiful but deadly maidens who fight with the fury of daemons. Above all other weapons the guard favour the repeater crossbows known as Uraithen (the Deathrain) and the Drannach (the Sky-Piercer), a long, heavy-bladed spear. The long years of discipline and war have honed these guard into the finest warriors in the world.

Do not scorn these citizen-soldiers, for they have won many a battle – and their lives are expendable should an occasion arise when you must sacrifice part of your army to achieve a victory in the name of King Malekith. Lead your army with conviction and brook no interference, but also do not overlook the pettier leaders who serve under you. Make your orders well known to the nobles and lordlings who bow to your command, that they may more effectively take to the field and execute your strategy.

Fight well and bring victory to the Druchii and you shall know how great are the rewards for good service under the inspired rule of Malekith. Waste his soldiers, bring dishonour and shame upon our people and you shall know that as our chosen King can be grateful, so too shall he avenge himself on those that fail him.

	M	WS	BS	S	T	W	I	A	Ld
Highborn	5	7	6	4	3	3	8	4	10
Noble	5	6	6	4	3	2	7	3	9
Lordling	5	4	4	3	3	1	5	2	8
Warrior	5	4	4	3	3	1	5	1	8

Special Rules
Hate High Elves: All Dark Elves are bitter enemies of their kin in Ulthuan and *hate* all High Elves (see page 84-85 of the Warhammer rulebook for the rules for hatred).

SORCERESSES

An army of Druchii does not fight with silvered steel alone, for there are other powerful forces which can be bent to the will of a brave army general. Call upon the Convents of the Sorceresses and entreat their aid, for their magical prowess will blight the warriors of the opposing army, scorch their souls from their bodies and bring ruination and curses aplenty upon their heads. Be careful in your dealings with these beautiful creatures though, for there is always a price to pay for their aid... always!

	M	WS	BS	S	T	W	I	A	Ld
High Sorceress	5	4	4	3	3	3	5	1	9
Sorceress	5	4	4	3	3	2	5	1	8

Special Rules
Sect Enmity: Use of magic is distasteful to the followers of Khaine, and there is a centuries-long feud between the Temple of Khaine and the Convents of the Sorceresses. The two factions distrust each other greatly. For this reason a Sorceress may never join a unit which contains an Assassin.

HAR GANETH EXECUTIONERS

When talking about the warriors you can muster from amongst the population, it is worthwhile to discuss the city of Har Ganeth, known as the Cursed Place by the slaves who are sent there. This city is devoted to the service of our great god Khaine in his aspect as the Executioner. Here the craft of Death is held in the highest esteem. The elite warriors of this city are the Executioners, and they are foremost amongst the warriors of the Witch King. Always ensure you deal well with the lords of Har Ganeth, for no Druchii wishes to feel his neck caressed by their deadly blades.

	M	WS	BS	S	T	W	I	A	Ld
Executioner	5	5	4	3	3	1	5	1	8
Draich-master	5	5	4	3	3	1	5	2	8

Special Rules
Killing Blow: Executioners are skilled in the use of their deadly blades, able to deliver a fatal hit to even the largest of foes. Executioners have the Killing Blow special rule (see page 112 of the Warhammer rulebook).

BLACK GUARD

If you are called upon to fight directly for the lordly Malekith, he may deign to send you a contingent of his personal guard. These are the Black Guard, the soldiery of our capital Naggarond, and they are the fiercest fighters in all of the Land of Chill. Wondrously ruthless and efficient on the attack, and immovable in defence, the Black Guard are the terror of our enemies. However, do not misuse their abilities, for they owe loyalty only to the mighty Witch King himself, and should they judge you to be at fault, you will answer to their deadly captain, Kouran. Such unpleasantness is to be avoided if you value your life and soul.

	M	WS	BS	S	T	W	I	A	Ld
Black Guard	5	5	4	3	3	1	6	1	9
Master	5	5	4	3	3	1	6	2	9

Special Rules

Hatred: Black Guard are vicious killers and *hate* everybody and everything (see page 84-85 of the Warhammer rulebook for the rules for hatred).

Stubborn: Raised from birth to protect the Witch King himself, Black Guard would rather die than give ground. Black Guard are *stubborn* (see page 85 of the Warhammer rulebook).

DARK RIDERS

Ahead of the armies of Druchii ride the heralds of Naggaroth, the dreaded Dark Riders who will serve as your eyes and ears. They are masters of sudden attacks and daring raids, scouring the land in search of the foe, laying ambushes for their supply trains and attacking with deadly speed against their reinforcements.

Dark Riders are experts in the use of repeater crossbows, long cavalry spears and wickedly curved swords. They ride fierce dark steeds taken from the stables of Ellyrion, reared and brought to heel by the Beastmasters. There is a poetic justice to this; where the Ellyrian weaklings dilute the natural fierceness and spirit of their steeds, our Beastmasters bring it out with their whips and hot brands.

	M	WS	BS	S	T	W	I	A	Ld
Dark Rider	5	4	4	3	3	1	5	1	8
Herald	5	4	5	3	3	1	5	1	8
Dark Steed	9	3	0	3	3	1	4	1	5

Special Rules

Fast Cavalry: Dark Riders follow the rules given for fast cavalry on page 117 of the Warhammer rulebook.

SHADES

While most of our folk live in the security of our fortified cities one of the clans, the Shades of the Blackspine Mountains, is a notable exception. The Shades are a silent and deadly brotherhood of warriors who guard the mountain passes to the west. They live apart from the rest of Dark Elf society, waging an endless war against the enemies of Malekith.

Many noble and proud warrior traditions of Nagarythe are kept alive by these mountain warriors, including the custom in which the newborn are treated. When an infant is born, its parents will leave it outside their tent for the first night of its life, and only if it survives is it deemed fit to be raised amongst the Shades. Use the Shadow Brotherhood as your scouts and infiltrators, for none are more adept at the art of infiltration and reconnaissance.

When the enemy is found and battle joined, your Shades should harass them with their withering crossbow fire, disrupting their attack and leaving them easy prey for the rest of your army.

	M	WS	BS	S	T	W	I	A	Ld
Shade	5	4	4	3	3	1	5	1	8
Bloodshade	5	4	5	3	3	1	5	1	8

Special Rules

Scouts: Shades can move effortlessly and unseen through enemy lines. Shades are Scouts (see page 112 of the Warhammer rulebook).

Skirmishers: Shades fight in a loose formation, and follow the rules for Skirmishers, (see page 115 of the Warhammer rulebook).

COLD ONE KNIGHTS

The nobles of the Druchii ride to battle atop ancient reptiles known as Cold Ones. Only very few of us can take up the arms of the Cold One Knights, for the lizards savagely attack all who come near them, recognising warm-blooded creatures by their smell. To avoid this the Cold One Knights anoint themselves with the poisonous slime of the Cold Ones so the beasts will accept them. There is a great price to pay though, for the poison numbs the senses so that the riders can no longer taste food or feel a touch. But it is a price worth paying, for the charge of the Cold One cavalry can shatter even the strongest enemy line.

A fully armed and armoured Cold One Knight carries a long lance known as a Kheitain (Soul Eater), wears a reinforced helm and full-length armour, and on his arm is slung a shield carrying the device of his house. Though they are few in number, the charge of the Cold One Knights is a decisive weapon which can win you the battle at a crucial moment.

	M	WS	BS	S	T	W	I	A	Ld
Knight	5	5	4	3	3	1	5	1	8
Dread Knight	5	5	4	3	3	1	5	2	8
Cold One	7	3	0	4	4	1	3	1	3

Special Rules

Fear: Cold Ones are monstrous reptiles which cause *fear*. See page 81 of the Warhammer rulebook for details.

Stupidity: Cold Ones are subject to *stupidity*. See page 82 of the Warhammer rulebook for details.

Thick-skinned: Cold Ones have thick scaly skin, which acts like armour and makes them difficult to injure. A warrior mounted on a Cold One counts +2 to his armour save instead of the normal +1 for being mounted.

COLD ONE CHARIOT

It is a symbol of great prestige to ride into battle upon the magnificent chariots of Naggarond. These are given as gifts to warriors who have pleased our lord Malekith with their devotion, bravery and prowess in battle. Accompanied by the roars of the Cold Ones and the thunder of wheels across the battlefield, a chariot smashing into the enemy is a sight magnificent to behold. Until recently the Witch King himself rode to battle in such fashion and, although in his wisdom our King has now renounced his decree for the Great Reclamation of our homeland, he once ruled that only he and no other was worthy of such a mount.

	M	WS	BS	S	T	W	I	A	Ld
Chariot	–	–	–	5	5	4	–	–	–
Crew	–	4	4	3	–	–	5	1	8
Cold One	7	3	–	4	–	–	3	1	–

Special Rules

Chariots: All rules governing chariots apply to Cold One Chariots (see pages 126-128 of the Warhammer rulebook).

Fear: A Cold One Chariot causes *fear* and has a Unit Strength of 4.

Stupidity: Cold Ones are subject to the rules for *stupidity*. Note that you use the Leadership value of the crew for Stupidity tests.

HARPIES

If you ever visit the distant city of Karond Kar, you will witness a spectacle that will fill you with elation and fear in equal measure. Upon the thermals of the sacrificial pyres soar the Harpies – winged beasts with a savage, primeval beauty. Some claim they are the souls of slain Witch Elves given form, others that they are a manifestation of Khaine in his aspect of the predator. They are creatures of Khaine, that is for sure, for they delight in the tormenting of their victims and feast upon raw flesh. The Harpy is a sign of good fortune and it is claimed that if they were ever to desert the city, it would fall to the enemy within ninety days.

	M	WS	BS	S	T	W	I	A	Ld
Harpy	4	3	3	3	3	1	4	1	6

Special Rules

Beasts: Harpies can never be joined or led by characters. They cannot use the General's Leadership value even if he is within 12".

Flying Unit: Harpies are a unit of flyers and follow the rules presented on page 106 of the Warhammer rulebook.

THE DARK FLEET

At the core of our navy are the Black Arks, the great floating fortresses protected by the sorcerous wards of our wizardry. Each Black Ark garrisons an army of Corsairs, and is well equipped with the deadly Reaper bolt throwers. Alongside them are the smaller vessels, the skiffs and slave-powered galleys which bring our warriors rapidly to the shore or to board an enemy ship. Great creatures from the depths are raised above the waves by the chilling calls of the Beastmasters, and atop the sea serpents and kraken our artisans raise defensive towers and shooting galleries.

CORSAIRS

To be a Corsair is a great honour amongst the Druchii, and it is a chance to win riches and fame and capture slaves during their raids, for one tenth of the loot captured by a Corsair belongs to him. Four tenths go to his captain and the remainder is the possession of the Witch King. These seafaring reavers excel at boarding other vessels, making them amongst our deadliest fighters in close combat.

	M	WS	BS	S	T	W	I	A	Ld
Corsair	5	4	4	3	3	1	5	1	8
Reaver	5	4	4	3	3	1	5	2	8

REAPER BOLT THROWER

Reaper bolt throwers are a testimony to the genius of our race. A mechanism of counterweights and strings allows this war machine to shoot a hail of barbed bolts, or a single missile with much greater force.

Reapers can be used at sea to clear the decks of enemy vessels, and on land to scythe down entire ranks of enemy warriors. The bolts of the Reaper are barbed and thus difficult to remove from wounds, causing great agony and torment for those unfortunate enough not to die. However, such casualties often suffer such horrendous injuries that they are worthless as slaves and are best left to bleed to death or given over to the bloody caresses of the Witch Elves.

The Reaper Bolt Thrower is a war machine and all the rules governing war machines apply. Reaper Bolt Throwers may either shoot a single bolt (follow the rules given on page 124 of the Warhammer rulebook) or they may fire multiple shots.

If using the multiple shots option then the Reaper Bolt Thrower shoots six bolts in each Shooting phase. These shots are worked out exactly like shots from bows or crossbows, using the Ballistic Skill of the crew to determine whether the bolts hit or not. All bolts must be directed towards a single target. Multiple shots have a Range of 48", a Strength of 4, with armour saves suffering a -2 penalty.

	M	WS	BS	S	T	W	I	A	Ld
Crew	5	4	4	3	3	1	5	1	8
Reaper	–	–	–	–	7	3	–	–	–

DEVOTEES OF KHAINE

In honour of our great god Khaela Mensha Khaine, the bloody-handed god of war and death, we have built mighty temples across our lands. Here the chosen brides of Khaine, the Witch Elves, practice the ancient rites and sacrifices under the watchful eyes of the Hag Queens. Each of our cities has a temple, and the rulers are required to pay a tithe to the Hag ruling over the Witch Elves within the temple. One slave in ten that our raiders bring back to Naggarond belongs to the Temple, where a great honour awaits them as they are sacrificed to Khaine. After opening their chests with knives purified by dark venom, the Hags bathe in their blood to restore their pact with the Lord of Murder. Few slaves understand or appreciate this great privilege.

WITCH ELVES

Witch Elves are the maiden-elves who are wedded to Khaine, the Lord of Murder, in midnight rites of blood sacrifice and magic. The decadent, fragile looks of the maidens of Ulthuan are nothing compared to the intoxicating beauty of the Witch Elves. Many are willing to die (and, indeed, often do) to see but a smile on the blood-red lips of the Witch Elves. Do not desire the touch of a Maibd, a bride of Khaine, for her life is wholly given to the Lord of Murder, and he is a jealous god, unwilling to share his chosen ones.

Witch Elves go to war alongside the armies of our noble King, eager to prove themselves in the eyes of their god. For them the battlefield is just another temple of Khaine, and the screams of the dying are praises sung in honour of the bloody-handed god. Before battle, the Brides of Khaine drink blood laced with drugs which fills them with bloodlust and rage. Then they throw themselves at the enemy, showing them the foolishness of opposing the Druchii.

	M	WS	BS	S	T	W	I	A	Ld
Witch Elf	5	5	4	3	3	1	6	1	8
Hag	5	5	4	3	3	1	6	2	8

Special Rules

Poisoned Attacks: Witch Elf blades are often coated with noxious venoms. They have Poisoned Attacks as described on page 114 of the Warhammer rulebook.

Frenzy: Witch Elves (including Hags) are affected by the rules for *frenzy* as detailed on page 84 of the Warhammer rulebook.

Devotees of Khaine: With the exception of an Assassin, no Dark Elf character may join a unit of Witch Elves. It's not that they don't trust the Witch Elves… well, actually it is.

CAULDRON OF BLOOD

A Cauldron of Blood is an ancient artefact of the long-gone days when the gods walked the earth. It is a gift from Khaine, the Lord of Murder, and within it lies the secret of eternal youth and beauty. A bride of Khaine may bathe in the blood-filled Cauldron, and it will renew her vitality and youth. The few Cauldrons that *have survived the millennia are kept at the great temple of Ghrond, guarded by the High Priestesses of the Cult. One may be brought out to battle, but only in times of great bloodshed when the Witch Elf sect fights in strength.*

THE CAULDRON IN THE GAME

The Cauldron and its Guardians are considered to be a single entity and have a Unit Strength of 3. The Cauldron cannot move and its Guardians must remain within 2" of it. The Cauldron itself cannot be harmed. Any shooting hits scored against the unit are divided evenly between the Guardians. The energies of Khaine surround the Cauldron, giving the guardians a 4+ Ward save against missile fire (including *magic missiles*), and Magic Resistance (1).

In hand-to-hand combat the guardians are assembled in front of the Cauldron in the same way as a war engine crew, fighting with any enemies in base contact. The Cauldron cannot be attacked. The Guardians cannot be broken in combat.

If all of the Guardians are killed, the Cauldron is considered destroyed.

Terror: The Cauldron of Blood is surrounded by an aura of bloodshed, and causes *terror*.

Red Fury: Any Dark Elf units (including the Guardians) within 18" of the Cauldron of Blood are driven into a fury of destruction by the Cauldron's presence. Affected units may re-roll failed rolls to wound in the first round of any combat. In addition, affected Witch Elf units are always *frenzied* – if within 18" they cannot lose their *frenzy*, if they have lost their *frenzy* and move within 18" they regain it immediately. The baleful energies seeping from the Cauldron give all Witch Elves within 18" of it a 6+ Ward save.

ASSASSINS

During the revelries of the Death Night, the Witch Elves roam the streets of our cities, and all who cross their path are offerings to Khaine. Amongst those taken are young babes, who are offered up to the Lord of Murder in the Cauldron of Blood. Most perish, but those chosen by Khaine emerge unharmed, and are then initiated in the dark secrets of Khaine. They are raised to be Dark Elf Assassins, the masters of death and the bringers of oblivion.

All Assassins follow one of the aspects of Khaine, the thousand-faced god of murder, and under his patronage their powers grow unrivalled by mere mortals. They become masters of the martial arts and learn the power of poisons. They are one of the most potent tools in the armoury of the Witch King, and those lords foolish enough to question their loyalty to Malekith disappear swiftly.

Each Assassin strives to become more like our god. The rivalry between Assassins is fierce, and all of them are constantly developing new killing techniques. There are no greater warriors amongst all Elvenkind than the Adepts of Khaine.

	M	WS	BS	S	T	W	I	A	Ld
Assassin	6	9	9	4	3	2	10	3	10

Hidden: If you wish, any Assassin in your army may start the game hidden in one of the following units: Witch Elves, Warriors, Corsairs, Executioners or Black Guard.

Hidden Assassins are not placed on the table, but are assumed to move along with whatever unit they are with. At the start of the game, make a note of which unit they are hidden in. If the unit is wiped out or flees off the table before the Assassin is revealed then the Assassin is lost and Victory points are scored as normal. Before he is revealed, there is no other way the Assassin can be harmed.

Hidden Assassins may be revealed at the beginning of any of your turns or at the start of any Close Combat phase. The player declares that his unit contains an Assassin and places the model amongst the ranks where he can fight, displacing a normal rank-and-file model. If there are no such models in the front rank, the Assassin is placed in the second rank until there is enough room for him in the first rank. Assassins always strike first in the round of hand-to-hand combat they are revealed, even against chargers. If an enemy model is also entitled to always strike first, the model with higher Initiative strikes first (roll a D6 if they have equal Initiative).

Leadership: Assassins are not great leaders, but are ruthless and highly disciplined warriors. Units in the Dark Elf army can never use their Leadership value and an Assassin can never be the General of the army (therefore your army must include at least one other character to act as the General).

BEASTS OF KAROND KAR

Karond Kar is the bastion of our Beastmasters. Here are the stables where the beasts that serve our great cause are reared and trained, and where the stolen steeds brought up by the soft Ellyrians are brought to bear by whip and red-hot brand. The folk of Karond Kar also tame the ferocious Cold Ones, hatch and hand rear the beasts and train them to accept riders.

BEASTMASTERS

Since the distant days of Nagarythe, our folk have been experts at bending beasts and animals to our will. However, some show exceptional aptitude in this, and can command even the unruliest beasts with a single word. They are the famed Beastmasters. When a child shows talent for taming animals he is sent to the city of Karond Kar to study under the masters who dwell there.

The Beastmasters are also in charge of the slaves, for humans, Orcs and their like are no more than beasts themselves. Beastmasters are experts at getting the most out of their stock, and are always chosen from amongst the most robust and resourceful of our folk.

	M	WS	BS	S	T	W	I	A	Ld
Beastmaster	5	4	4	3	3	2	6	2	8

Special Rules

Beastmaster: Any monster taking a Monster Reaction test within 12" of a Beastmaster may re-roll the required Leadership test once. If a Beastmaster is slain whilst riding a monster, the monster does not need to take a Monster Reaction test and will fight on as normal.

WAR HYDRA

The War Hydra is a titanic monster, a creature from the dark caverns below the Blackspine Mountains. It is a fearsome, scaled beast with many serpentine heads that belch smoke and fire and rend men with their sharp fangs. Since ages past we have trained the Hydras to be used in war to break the lines of the enemy troops with their massive bulk and fiery breath. The Beastmasters of Karond Kar continually experiment with different breeds and use magic to bring the natural ferocity of these beasts to new heights.

	M	WS	BS	S	T	W	I	A	Ld
War Hydra	6	4	0	5	5	6	2	5	6
Apprentice	5	4	4	3	3	1	5	1	8

Special Rules

Scaly Skin: War Hydras have a scaly skin which gives them a 4+ armour save.

Large creature: A War Hydra is a titanic creature and counts as a large target.

Breathe Fire: The heads of the War Hydra can breathe fire in the Shooting phase. Use the teardrop-shaped template to determine which troops are hit, exactly like any other breath weapon. Hits are resolved at Strength 3, and are flaming attacks.

Controlled: Each War Hydra is driven into battle by two Beastmaster Apprentices who direct it with lashes and long-tined goads. The two Apprentices must remain within 1" of the War Hydra at all times. If the Apprentices are killed, the War Hydra must make a Monster Reaction test just like a ridden monster which loses its rider. A Beastmaster on foot may join the unit (replacing a lost Apprentice if you wish), but once the Hydra has taken a Monster Reaction test it always operates as an independent model. No other model may join a Hydra/Apprentice unit.

Any shooting against the unit gains the +1 to hit modifier for a large target. If there are any Apprentices visible to the firing unit, roll a D6 for each hit. On a roll of 1 to 4, the Hydra is hit, on a roll of 5 or 6 an Apprentice is hit. If there is no line of sight to the Apprentices then all hits are worked out on the Hydra (so it's a good idea to hide them behind it in your movement phases!)

In close combat, the War Hydra and any surviving Apprentices are arranged just like a skirmishing unit and models fight with opponents in base contact as normal. The Apprentices are adept at using the bulk of the Hydra to protect themselves, so that all enemies who can choose to attack them or the Hydra must allocate their attacks against the Hydra. The unit may only charge enemies which the War Hydra could normally charge (within a 90° arc to its front).

Terror: The War Hydra is a huge and frightening monster which causes *terror* as detailed on pages 81-82 of the Warhammer rulebook.

MANTICORE

You should hold no creature in higher esteem than the Manticore, for it is one of the thousand aspects of our Lord Khaine. With the body of a titanic lion, larger than any of the predators of the mountains, wings of a huge bat, whip-like tail, and fury to match that of Khaine himself, Manticores reign supreme in the mountains of our northern border.

Manticores are sacred beasts, captured, reared and trained by the Beastmasters as steeds for the lords of Naggaroth, for in battle they can unleash the fury of the Bloody-handed god upon our enemies. Beastmasters often ride these majestic beasts themselves, as proof that they can break the will of these most unruly of creatures.

	M	WS	BS	S	T	W	I	A	Ld
Manticore	6	5	0	5	5	4	5	4	5

Special Rules

Fly: A Manticore has huge, bat-like wings and may *fly* as described on page 106 of the the Warhammer Rulebook.

Terror: The Manticore is a titanic, enraged beast which causes *terror* as detailed on pages 81-82 of the Warhammer rulebook.

Large Target: The Manticore is huge monster and so is therefore a large target.

DARK PEGASUS

Dark Pegasi are favoured mounts of the Sorceresses, found amongst the peaks of the highest mountains. They are ferocious hunters in the wilds, a trait which can easily be turned to useful purpose in our armies.

	M	WS	BS	S	T	W	I	A	Ld
Dark Pegasus	8	3	0	4	4	3	4	2	6

Special Rules

Fly: A Dark Pegasus has leathery wings and may *fly* as described in the Warhammer rulebook.

Impale: A Dark Pegasus uses its horns to impale its prey. A Dark Pegasus attacks at +1 Strength when charging.

BLACK DRAGON

The great wyrms that slumber under the peaks of the Blackspine Mountains are dark in their hue. No one knows for sure the origin of these ancient serpents. Some say that they are hatchlings of the Dragon eggs taken from the ancient nests of Caledor that were then reared by the Beastmasters, while others claim that they are servants of Khaine sent to this world. Only the greatest lords amongst the Dark Elves ride to battle atop one of these monsters which, even alone, have the power to break the back of an army.

	M	WS	BS	S	T	W	I	A	Ld
Black Dragon	6	6	0	6	6	6	3	5	8

Special Rules

Fly: Black Dragons have wings and may *fly* as described on page 106 of the Warhammer rulebook.

Large Target: A Black Dragon is an enormous mass of fang, muscle and scale and therefore counts as a large target.

Noxious Breath: The Black Dragon can breathe corrosive and poisonous fumes which can burn skin and hair, and choke a man to death.

This is a breath weapon (see page 114 of the Warhammer rulebook). Hits are resolved with a Strength of 4 and any unit taking casualties from the noxious breath must pass a Leadership test in order to declare charges next turn.

Undead and Daemons are not affected by this additional penalty, nor are troops that are immune to psychology, although they still suffer damage as normal.

Scaly Skin: The iron-hard skin of the Black Dragon gives it a 3+ armour save.

Terror: A Black Dragon is a huge monster which causes *terror* as detailed on pages 81-82 of the Warhammer rulebook.

THE DARK ART

Only by the divine will of the Witch King is a Druchii allowed to study the high art of magic. It is the vitality and power of our magic which sustains us, destroys our enemies and empowers our Black Arks.

Those who succeed in the twelve tests of a Sorceress are found worthy and embrace the Dark Art in all its majesty. They become members of one of the six Convents of Sorceresses, ever ready to serve the Witch King. Those who fail and yet survive will serve the cause of Lord Malekith in more menial ways as mindless slaves.

A Sorceress must walk the dark paths of the Realm of Chaos, the deep pits of the oceans, and the raging bowels of the fiery mountains in her quest for knowledge. The channelling of the raw Winds of Chaos and the binding of these forces give the Sorceress her power. The creatures of the Chaos Hells will bow to her will in the end. Such power is vast but dangerous, and the aspirant to the Dark Convent of the Sorceresses must be courageous and strong. She must be wedded first and foremost to the great Witch King, and so may never take a husband nor sire children. Thus also, the Witch King is alone among our fathers and forefathers able to wield the powers of the Darkest Abyss.

From the Sixth Book of Secrets by Kaladhtoir of Clar Karond

USING THE DARK ART IN YOUR GAMES

Dark Elf Sorcerers and Sorceresses may use either the Dark Magic spell list or one of the following spell lores from the Warhammer rulebook: Shadow or Death. They may only pick spells from a single list.

All practitioners of the Dark Arts are incredibly adept at manipulating the Winds of Magic in their rawest form, channelling energies that would disintegrate lesser beings. A Dark Elf magic user therefore adds +1 to all of their casting rolls.

'And lo, he shall rule with a dark hand and his shadow shall touch upon every land. Steel will be his skin and fire will be his blood, in hatred will be conquer all before him. No blade forged of Man, Dwarf or Elf shall endure him fear. Though will it come to pass that the firstborn son of noble blood shall rise to power. The child will be learned in the darkest arts and he will raise an army of terrible beasts. Thus will the Dark King fall, slain by neither blade nor arrow but by a sorcerous power of darkest magic and so shall his body be consumed in the flames and for all eternity burn.'

The Prophecy of Demise

As Aenarion drew the Blade of Khaine, Caledor was gifted with a prophecy which spoke of the tragedy that would befall Elvenkind. Part of the prophecy talks of a great warrior cast from his home by a Sorcerer and Malekith believes it is he to whom the prophecy refers. As a result Sorcerers are regarded with disdain, fear and superstition by most Dark Elves, and they cannot be admitted to the Convent. There are those in Naggaroth, however, who will employ such magic users to avoid owing a debt to the High Sorceresses of the Convent.

Dark Magic

To randomly generate a spell from the Dark Art list, roll a D6 and consult the chart below. If you roll the same spell twice for the same Wizard roll again. Any Sorceress can automatically swap one spell for Chillwind if you wish.

D6	Spell	Difficulty
1	**Nagaelythe the Chillwind**	5+
2	**Doombolt of Kharaidon**	6+
3	**Chroesh – Word of Pain**	8+
4	**Anchan-Rogar the Soul Stealer**	9+
5	**Lamehk's Dominion**	10+
6	**Arnizipal's Black Horror**	12+

CHILLWIND — Difficulty 5+

Calling upon the coldness of Nagaelythe of the Utterdark, the Dark Elf unleashes a freezing wind against their enemies. Chillwind is a *magic missile* with a range of up to 24". The spell causes D6 Strength 3 hits, and a unit which suffers any casualties may do nothing in the next Shooting phase due to numbing coldness.

DOOMBOLT — Difficulty 6+

As the invocation is spoken, the otherworldy beast known as Kharaidon unleashes a bolt of pure darkness upon the Dark Elves' adversaries. Doombolt is a *magic missile* with a range of up to 18". If successfully cast the Doombolt hits its target and causes D6 Strength 5 hits.

WORD OF PAIN
Remains in Play — Difficulty 8+

Upon uttering the true name of Khaine as the Serpent Lord, an unnatural and unbearable agony suffuses the body of his hated foes. This spell can be cast on an enemy unit which is within 24" and is visible to the caster. Any models in the unit have their Weapon Skill and Ballistic Skill reduced to 1. Once it is cast the Word of Pain remains in play until the wizard chooses to end it (which she can do at any time), it is dispelled, she attempts to cast another spell, or she is slain.

SOUL STEALER — Difficulty 9+

The daemon-crawler Anchan-Rogar reaches out from his domain and plucks the souls from the enemy. Nominate one enemy unit within 6", which may be in close combat. Every model in the unit takes a Strength 3 hit. For each unsaved wound caused, the Sorceress gains one extra wound. The wizard may never have more than double their original number of Wounds, any extra are lost.

DOMINION — Difficulty 10+

Calling upon Lamehk the Slavemaster of the Third Hell, the wizard takes control of the foe's thoughts. This spell can be cast on an enemy unit within 12". In the following enemy turn the Dark Elf player may prohibit one of the unit's following actions: the move of the unit; the shooting of the unit; any Wizards in the unit casting spells.

Note that any Wizard in the unit still adds the normal number of Power dice to the opponent's pile even if he does not cast spells himself.

BLACK HORROR — Difficulty 12+

The wizard conjures a whirling vortex of Dark energy which drags her victims into one of the infernal regions. Place the large (5") template anywhere within line of sight and with the centre within 18" of the wizard. Any models completely under are automatically affected, models partially under are affected on a roll of 4+.

Affected models suffer a wound with no armour saves if the Dark Elf player can roll over the model's Strength on a D6 (rolls of 6 always succeed). Models without a normal Strength characteristic, such as war engines, are destroyed on a roll of a 6. Any unit that loses one or more Wounds must take an immediate Panic test.

SORCEROUS ITEMS

Dark Elves are a race touched by magic, and they are the ultimate masters of Dark Sorcery. Thus the armoury of the Witch King is filled with many blades woven with dire curses and black suits of armour ensorcelled with spells of resistance and protection. This section describes the rules for the ancient weapons and enchanted items used by the Dark Elves. They may be used by those models indicated in the army list. Note that all the rules on magic items presented on pages 152-153 of the Warhammer rulebook also apply to the 'Dark Elves only' magic items.

COMMON MAGIC ITEMS

SWORD OF STRIKING   **30 points**
Weapon; +1 To Hit.

SWORD OF BATTLE   **25 points**
Weapon; +1 Attack.

SWORD OF MIGHT   **20 points**
Weapon; +1 Strength.

BITING BLADE   **10 points**
Weapon; -1 armour save.

ENCHANTED SHIELD   **10 points**
Armour; 5+ armour save.

TALISMAN OF PROTECTION   **15 points**
Talisman; 6+ Ward save.

STAFF OF SORCERY   **50 points**
Arcane; +1 to dispel.

DISPEL SCROLL (one use only)   **25 points**
Arcane; Automatically dispel an enemy spell.

POWER STONE (one use only)   **25 points**
Arcane; +2 dice to cast a spell.

WAR BANNER   **25 points**
Banner; +1 Combat Resolution.

MAGIC WEAPONS

EXECUTIONER'S AXE   80 points

The Executioner's Axe is a huge black bladed weapon bound with spells of dismemberment. A single blow from it can cut any opponent in half.

When rolling to wound in close combat and for armour save modifier purposes, the wielder counts as having a Strength double that of his target's Toughness. However, the Executioner's Axe is two-handed and the wielder always strikes last except in the turn he charges.

VENOM SWORD   75 points

The Venom Sword is forged from the poison of a thousand malicious serpents. When it strikes, mystical poisons flow into the veins of its victim.

Any model which loses a wound to the Venom Sword (after saves, etc) must roll equal to or under its Toughness on 2D6 or is automatically slain.

BLADE OF RUIN   50 points

This magical sword can cleave through armour as if it were air.

No armour saves may be taken against hits from the Blade of Ruin. Ward saves may be taken as normal.

HYDRA BLADE   50 points

The Hydra Blade strikes repeatedly like its multi-headed namesake.

A character wielding the Hydra Blade gains D3 additional attacks (roll each Close Combat phase the Hydra Blade is used).

CRIMSON DEATH   35 points

This huge halberd was carried into battle by Dark Lord Khalak of Ghrond.

A warrior wielding Crimson Death always strikes with Strength 6. No other modifiers will ever reduce this. Requires two hands to use.

LIFETAKER   30 points

Lifetaker is a repeater crossbow fashioned from blackest steel, with bolts tipped with the venom of a black dragon.

Lifetaker is treated like an ordinary repeater crossbow, with the following additional rules. Lifetaker always hits on a 2+, regardless of To Hit modifiers. You may re-roll failed rolls to wound with Lifetaker. Remember that a dice can never be re-rolled more than once.

WEB OF SHADOWS   25 points
One use only.

Woven from the hair of the Witch Elves and studded with ensorcelled Harpy fangs, a victim caught in the Web of Shadows will be ripped to shreds.

A Web of Shadows can only be used once per game against a single enemy model. The character uses the Web of Shadows instead of making any normal attacks that round. When used, one model in base contact with the character automatically takes 2D6 Strength 3 hits. A character with a Web of Shadows may also use another ordinary close combat weapon (but not another magic weapon).

HEARTSEEKER   25 points

Heartseeker has the uncanny ability to find the heart of a living thing. Dark Elves delight in its ability to destroy the lifeforce of their victims.

The character may re-roll all missed attacks with Heartseeker. Remember a dice can never be re-rolled more than once.

CHILL BLADE   25 points

The blade of this sword holds a terrible spell of coldness which seeps into the Dark Elf's victim, freezing their soul and temporarily paralysing them.

Any model wounded by a Chill Blade (after saves, etc) may not attack for the rest of that combat round.

DARK SWORD   15 points

Etched upon the blade of this sword is an ancient curse in the Dark Tongue. Upon striking a foe, the curse is unleashed.

Any model losing one or more wounds (after saves, etc) to the Dark Sword becomes subject to the rules for *stupidity* for the remainder of the battle.

MAGIC ARMOUR

ARMOUR OF LIVING DEATH   100 points

It is claimed that anyone wearing this armour cannot die, that they are sustained by its magical energy. Unfortunately, they cannot remove the armour and are slowly driven insane.

The Armour of Living Death counts as heavy armour, giving a 5+ armour save, which can be combined with other armour as normal. In addition, the model has +1 Toughness and +1 Wound.

ARMOUR OF ETERNAL SERVITUDE   60 points

Oaths of loyalty and dedication to Khaine were sworn at the time of the armour's forging, and the wearer is granted extended life to serve his god.

This light armour gives a basic 6+ save, which can be combined with other armour as normal. In addition, the wearer can regenerate (see page 113 of the Warhammer rulebook).

SHIELD OF GHROND   30 points

Shaped into the leering face of an Ice Daemon, the shield of Ghrond is imbued with the power of the north wind which robs attacks of their force.

The Shield of Ghrond is treated like a normal shield, and in addition any hits the character suffers will be resolved with -1 Strength.

ARMOUR OF DARKNESS   25 points

Forged from black meteoric steel, this suit is almost impossible to pierce.

This armour includes a shield and gives a save of 2+ which cannot be improved in any way.

BLOOD ARMOUR   20 points

When anointed with the blood of the enemy, this armour becomes ever more endurable.

Blood Armour is treated as a suit of normal heavy armour (5+ save) and can be combined with other armour as normal. For every unsaved wound the wearer inflicts, their save is improved by 1 point (to 4+ then 3+, etc) up to a maximum of 1+.

TALISMANS

BLACK AMULET   50 points

Cast from the heartstone of a mountain tainted with the power of Dark Sorcery, the Black Amulet is a lustrous polished stone of midnight hue, engraved with a single glowing rune.

The wearer has a 5+ Ward save against close combat hits. If the wearer of the Black Amulet passes his Ward save then the attacking model suffers 1 wound instead. There is no save against such a rebounded wound, even from Wards.

DEATHMASK   50 points

Made of enchanted gold from the Blackspine Mountains, the Deathmask depicts Khaela Mensha Khaine in his aspect of the Deathbringer, the merciless slayer.

The wearer of the mask causes *terror*.

CROWN OF BLACK IRON   35 points

Made by Furion of Clar Karond, the Crown of Iron captures Dark Magic and oozes a sinister daemonic shadow which protects the wearer.

The character has a 5+ Ward save. In addition to this, the wearer is completely immune to the effects of Light Magic and High Magic spells. Note that this is not a Dispel and thus other models (excluding the character's mount) may be affected by High Magic and Light Magic.

SEAL OF GHROND   25 points

This iron seal carries the rune of Khaine in his aspect of the Iron Panther, the stalker of the void.

The seal of Ghrond adds one dice to the Dispel dice pool of the army.

RING OF HOTEK   20 points

Hotek, the renegade priest of Vaul, made this ring to protect himself from the magical forces used in the forging of his artifacts.

Any magic user (friend or foe) attempting to cast a spell within 6" of the wearer will miscast on the roll of any double. If they roll a double 6 they cast the spell (with Irresistible Force) and then suffer a Miscast.

ENCHANTED ITEMS

RUBRIC OF DARK DIMENSIONS   50 points
One use only. Models on foot only.
Bound spell. Power level 5.

By opening this device the bearer creates a gate into a dimension of pure evil.

All enemy models in base contact with the bearer must roll equal to or under their Strength on a D6 (6 always fails) or be sucked into the dimension of Eternal Nightmares (and count as slain!).

RING OF DARKNESS   45 points
Bound spell. Power level 4.
From the opal set into this ring emerges a billowing black smoke which engulfs its wearer.

Attacks in close combat against the wearer require a 6 to hit regardless of Weapon Skills and modifiers. Remains in play.

CRYSTAL OF MIDNIGHT   25 points
One use only.
Bound spell. Power level 4.
Inside this black glowing crystal is a malignant captured spirit that can be unleashed to seek out the mind of an enemy magic user and steal his thoughts.

Nominate a Wizard anywhere on the table. The Wizard must pass a Leadership test on 3D6 otherwise he forgets one randomly determined spell for the rest of the battle.

ARCANE ITEMS

SOULSTONE   25 points
This gem holds the tortured soul of a sacrificed wizard. If a Sorceress is in danger of losing control of her magic she can feed the captured soul to Daemons to save herself.

A Soulstone makes the Sorceress immune to the effects of her first Miscast. Note that a Miscast spell still fails regardless of the actual dice score rolled.

BLACK STAFF   20 points
A Black Staff is the talisman of one of the six High Mistresses of the Convents of Sorceresses.

There is no maximum number of Power dice the wielder can use to attempt a spell.

DARKSTAR CLOAK   20 points
Woven into the fabric of this cloak is the essence of a star stolen from the night sky of Nagarythe.

The cloak gives the Sorceress +1 Power dice in each of her own Magic phases. Only she may use this extra dice.

TOME OF FURION   15 points
Furion of Clar Karond inscribed this book onto sheets of flayed Orc skin to teach the Path of Darkness to the uninitiated.

The Tome of Furion grants its bearer one additional spell.

MAGIC STANDARDS

BANNER OF NAGARYTHE   150 points
The Banner of Nagarythe, the standard of northern Ulthuan that now lies beneath the ocean, is the personal banner of the Witch King, proclaiming his reign over the Elven kingdoms.

This standard adds +1 to the combat resolution of all friendly Dark Elf units within 6" and the unit carrying the banner is Unbreakable.

HYDRA BANNER   80 points
Imbued with the magic of the Hydra Queen, this banner quickens the reflexes so that those nearby strike with her own speed and savagery.

All models in the unit (including mounts) gain +1 Attack in the first round of any hand-to-hand combat.

DREAD BANNER   75 points
Such is the supernatural fear instilled by the visage of the Bloody-handed God upon this standard that few dare to even look at it.

The unit carrying this standard causes *fear*.

BANNER OF MURDER   45 points
This standard is steeped in the blood of sacrificial victims, its murderous aura instilling a thirst for death and carnage in those carrying it aloft.

The unit adds +D6" to its charge moves. Declare charges first and then roll. If the charge is failed the unit will move forward its normal failed charge distance

STANDARD OF SLAUGHTER   35 points
One use only.
Anointed with the blood of an Ulthuan Elf, this banner imbues the unit with a bitter determination.

The unit gains +D3 to its combat resolution the first time it charges.

Thick smoke rose from the twelve sacrificial temples of the city of Naggaroth, imbuing the entire city with its rich sweet odour. Today was the Harvest of Souls, one of the many festivals of dedication to their god Khaine. Each noble family would try to better their neighbours by sacrificing the most slaves. Those families who were generous in their donations would be blessed by the sisterhood and spared their wrath on Death Night. The Dark Elf children eagerly waited at the temple doors where the priestesses would hand them the severed heads of those slain. The young Elves would then race each other to stick their trophies upon spikes that bristled on the parapets of the high city walls.

Inside the temples, after disembowelling their victims and placing their hearts and entrails on the sacrificial pyres, the Witch Elves would remove their flesh and sew it together in large sheets. A family's status was measured by the size of these macabre decorations which would be draped along the length of the city walls. Blood flowed through the city streets but high above the frenzied debauchery Malekith sat, oblivious to the festivity below. He had witnessed countless celebrations of death and cared little about such matters.

From a window in the tallest tower of the city, the highest point in the whole of Naggarond, he turned his gaze towards the east. Naggarond was his land to do with as he chose. Each and every soul belonged to him and should he choose he could crush them at will, but it was not enough. Whilst his people revelled in their own self-indulgence his enemies grew stronger. Even now in Ulthuan the pathetic warriors of Eltharion boasted about how they had successfully led an army to the shores of Naggarond. Until then no mortal had set foot on his land without permission. This was a sign that his people were growing weak, decadent in their self-belief. Some blamed this on the growing influence of the underground cults. Even today whilst the people rejoiced through slaughter in the name of Khaine, there were those who preferred to place their faith with other gods. He cared not for such affairs; the backstabbing and internal politics of the Dark Elves served to strengthen his people. Amidst the poison and plotting, the weak would die in order that the strong prevail. Whilst such treachery thrived and blossomed, his race's hearts grew colder and harder, it was as he wished it to be.

Malekith turned from the window and strode over to his throne. Carved from the bones of those whom the Witch King had slain, blood flowed from the open sockets of skulls at the base of the dais. To the left of the throne rested a long sword with wicked barbed edges. It had been too long since he had wielded his weapon. Malekith felt his hatred of the High Elf race surge; his anger flared, raging like a wild fire it grew in intensity. Destroyer, his magic blade, would tonight taste blood again. As the fury coursed through his body it numbed the pain of his burns. His body had been horribly mutilated when he had attempted to pass through the sacred flame of Asuryan and even now Malekith found swamping his emotions in hatred was his only escape from the burning anguish. The bitter memory of his injuries intensified his desire to kill.

He strode purposefully to the balcony where his Black Dragon sat, woken from its sleep as it sensed the rising malice that was growing inside its master. Malekith mounted the steed and, without any word of command, the great beast launched itself off the balcony, plummeting to the ground like a hawk diving for prey, invisible through the thick smoke to those below. Master and beast let out a wrath-filled howl that sent a shiver of fear down the spine of even the Hag Queen herself. Each Dark Elf in the city knew that the Witch King was seeking vengeance. In the midst of festivity their master had declared that war was at hand and, as his people, they were bound to join him.

THE DARK ARMOURY

The following items are unique to the Dark Elf army, and are available to certain units as described in the army list (pages 26-32).

SEA DRAGON CLOAKS

The Corsairs of the Dark Elf fleet wear heavy cloaks fashioned from the scales of the mighty sea dragons which accompany the ships. The cloak can be drawn tightly around the body when being fired at, acting as shield against missile fire. A Sea Dragon cloak adds +1 to the model's save in close combat, and +2 against ranged attacks (including spells, etc). It may be combined with other types of armour.

REPEATER CROSSBOW

Used almost exclusively by the Dark Elves of Naggaroth, the repeater crossbow is a lighter, less powerful type of crossbow that has a magazine of bolts which allows a single bolt to drop into place ready for firing as the string is drawn. A repeater crossbow can fire a hail of shots in the time it takes to shoot one ordinary crossbow bolt.

Maximum range: 24"; **Strength:** 3

Rules: 2 x Multiple Shots

THE TEMPLE OF KHAINE

Many weapons and skills are unique to the disciples of Khaine. These are the most well-kept secrets of the Temple, and they are never taught to outsiders. Many of the blades carried by Assassins and Witch Elves have been envenomed, for the lore of poison is well understood in the Temples of Khaine.

Some models in the Dark Elf army are allowed to use one or more of the special equipment or skills detailed below. See individual army list entries for details. A model may not be given multiples of the same upgrade, but an upgrade can be taken by more than one character.

POISONS

Any normal weapon may be coated with one type of poison. Magic weapons may not be poisoned. Many of these poisons contain mystical ingredients, making them deadly even to creatures not of mortal flesh.

Manbane   25 points

Manbane is one of the most lethal venoms ever devised, causing even the tiniest wound to bleed openly.

A character with a weapon coated with Manbane always counts their Strength as one higher than their target's Toughness, unless their Strength would normally be more than this, up to a maximum of Strength 6. In effect, this means that they almost always wound opponents on a roll of 3+. This modified Strength is also used to calculate armour save modifiers.

Black Lotus   25 points

Black Lotus has a terrifying effect on living flesh, driving victims into delusions and insanity.

For every Wound a model suffers from a weapon poisoned with Black Lotus (after saves, etc) they also lose 1 point from all of their other characteristics except Movement. This lasts for the rest of the battle.

Dark Venom   10 points

Extracted from the poisonous reptiles of the bleak land of Naggaroth, Dark Venom is a deadly toxin. A weapon coated with Dark Venom will cause a mortal wound if it even merely scratches skin.

The model is considered to have Poisoned Attacks as detailed on page 114 of the Warhammer rulebook.

ARTIFACTS AND SKILLS

Dance of Doom   30 points

The sinuous Dance of Doom can enthral even the most steely disciplined Swordmaster and be used to dodge the fastest shot or blow.

The model has a 5+ Ward save.

Touch of Death   30 points

The Adepts of Death school the servants of Khaine to learn the points on a body which kill instantly.

The model has the Killing Blow special ability as described on page 112 of the Warhammer rulebook.

Rune of Khaine   25 points

The Hag Queens burn the rune of the Lord of Murder upon the brow of the most zealous of killers.
The Rune of Khaine grants +1 Attack to its bearer. A model marked with the Rune of Khaine must always pursue fleeing enemies.

Hand of Khaine   25 points

Tracing a complex pattern in the air, the Dark Elf entrances their victim, leaving him vulnerable and open to attack.

Any one model (chosen by a Dark Elf player) in base contact will lose one Attack. Against mounted models, the Dark Elf player must choose either the mount/monster or the rider. If the model has several types of attack (an extra bite, for example) the Dark Elf player chooses which type of attack is lost. Models which are immune to psychology are not affected by the Hand of Khaine.

Witchbrew   25 points
(Hags only)

Witch Brew is a noxious liquid, distilled from blood, that the Witch Elves drink before battle. It drives them into such an ecstasy of destruction that they pay no heed to the enemies' numbers and will fight on against impossible odds.

The Hag and her unit drink the Witchbrew before the battle. Enemy units cannot claim the +1 combat resolution bonuses for outnumbering, flank and rear attacks or higher ground.

Cry of War   10 points

By screeching one of the seventeen secret names of Khaine, the warrior freezes enemies with horror.

A unit charged by a warrior with a Cry of War must pass a Leadership test or reduce their Weapon Skill by -1 (to a minimum of 1) for the duration of that Close Combat phase.

Stefan wrapped a piece of ripped shirt around the small wound on his arm. He had heard of the legendary martial prowess of the Witch Elves and considered himself lucky to walk away with but a small scratch. The wound was beginning to itch but Stefan thought nothing of it; he was exceptionally tired and though he fought to stay awake his eyes closed and he slowly slipped from consciousness. As he slept his dreams turned to haunting nightmares. Small black, sprite-like beings surrounded him tearing at his body, entering his mouth as he breathed. They attacked him, surrounding his prone body in a dark swarm of menacing lights. Try as he might, he could not fight them, they were too fast and there were too many of them. He tried to run from his attackers but his feet would not respond. Slowly the swarm suffocated him and he was helpless against them.

Johann stood at Stefan's doorway. He desperately needed fresh air to repress the nauseous feeling that had taken control of his entire body. He had been the one to discover Stefan's body. He knew the image of his friend would haunt him forever – it had swollen to twice its normal size and his clawed hands reached out as if trying to fend off some mysterious attacker. Johann had heard of the terrible effects of Black Lotus; he prayed that, when his time came, death would be swift.

ARMIES OF NAGGAROTH

The purpose of an army list is to enable players with vastly different armies to stage games which are as fair and evenly balanced as it is possible to make them. The army list gives each individual model a points value which represents its capabilities on the tabletop. The higher a model's points value the better it is in one or more respects: stronger, tougher, faster, better Leadership, and so on. The value of the army is simply the value of all the models added together.

As well as providing points costs, the list also divides the army into its constituent units. The list describes the weapons and optional equipment that troops can have and occasionally restricts the number of very powerful units an army can include. It would be very silly indeed if an army were to consist entirely of Reaper Bolt Throwers, or monstrous Hydras. The resulting game would be a frustrating and unbalanced affair, if not a complete waste of time. We employ army lists to ensure that this does not happen!

HOW THE ARMY LIST IS INTENDED TO BE USED

The army lists enable two players to choose armies of equal points value to fight a battle, as described in the main body of the Warhammer rules. The following list has been constructed with this purpose in mind.

The list can also be used when playing specific scenarios, either those described in the Warhammer rulebook, or others, including ones invented by the players. In this case, the list provides a framework which the players can adapt as required. It might, for example, be felt necessary to increase or decrease the number of characters or units allowed, or to restrict or remove options in the standard list such as magic items or monstrous mounts. If you refer to the Scenarios section of the Warhammer rulebook (pages 196-213), you'll find some examples of this kind.

ARMY LIST ORGANISATION

The army list is divided into four sections:

CHARACTERS

Characters represent the most able, skilled and successful individuals in your army: extraordinary leaders such as Nobles and Sorceresses. These form a vital and potent part of your forces.

CORE UNITS

These units are the most common warriors. They usually form the bulk of the army and will often bear the brunt of the fighting.

SPECIAL UNITS

Special units are the best of your warriors and include common engines of war. They are available to your army in limited numbers.

RARE UNITS

Rare units are so called because they are scarce compared to your ordinary troops. They represent unique units, uncommon creatures and unusual machines.

CHOOSING AN ARMY

Both players choose armies to the same agreed points value. Most players find that 2,000 points is about right for a battle that will last over an evening. Whatever value you agree, this is the maximum number of points you can spend. You can spend less and will probably find it is impossible to use up every last point. Most 2,000 points armies will therefore be something like 1,998 or 1,999 points, but they are still '2,000' points armies for our purposes. Once you have decided on a total points value, it is time to choose your force.

Choosing Characters

Characters are divided into two broad categories: Lords (the most powerful characters) and Heroes (the rest). The maximum number of characters an army can include is shown on the chart below.

Army Points Value	Max. Total Characters	Max. Lords	Max. Heroes
Less than 2,000	3	0	3
2,000 or more	4	1	4
3,000 or more	6	2	6
4,000 or more	8	3	8
Each +1,000	+2	+1	+2

An army does not have to include the maximum number of characters allowed, it can always include fewer than indicated. **However, an army must always include at least one character: the General.** An army does not have to include Lords, it can include all of its characters as Heroes if you prefer. At the start of the battle, choose one of the characters to be the General and make sure that you let your opponent know which one it is.

For example, a 2,500 points army could include a Noble (Lord), a Sorceress (Hero), an Assassin (Hero), and a Beastmaster (Hero) (ie, four characters in total, of which one is a Lord).

Choosing Troops

Troops are divided into Core, Special and Rare units. The number of each type of unit available depends on the army's points value, indicated on the chart below.

Army Points Value	Core Units	Special Units	Rare Units
Less than 2,000	2+	0-3	0-1
2,000 or more	3+	0-4	0-2
3,000 or more	4+	0-5	0-3
4,000 or more	5+	0-6	0-4
Each +1,000	+1 minimum	+0-1	+0-1

In some cases other limitations may apply to a particular kind of unit. This is specified in the unit entry. For example, the Black Guard Rare unit entry is accompanied by a note explaining that a maximum of one unit of this kind can be included in the army.

Unit Entries

Each unit is represented by an entry in the army list. The unit's name is given and any limitations that apply are explained.

Profiles. The characteristic profiles for the troops in each unit are given in the unit entry. Where several profiles are required, these are also given even if, as in many cases, they are optional.

Unit Sizes. Each entry specifies the minimum size for each unit. In the case of Core units this is usually 10 models. In the case of other units it is usually less. There are exceptions as you will see. In some cases, units also have a maximum size.

Weapons and Armour. Each entry lists the standard weapons and armour for that unit type. The value of these items is included in the points value. Additional or optional weapons and armour cost extra and are covered in the Options section of the unit entry.

Options. Lists the different weapon, armour and equipment options for the unit and any additional points cost for taking them. It may also include the option to upgrade a unit member into a Champion. While this model usually has a specific name (the Champion of a Witch Elf unit is called a Hag, for example) all the rules that apply to Champions apply to them. See the appropriate section of the Warhammer rulebook for details (pages 108-109).

Special Rules. Many troops have special rules which are fully described elsewhere in this book. These rules are also summarised for your convenience in the army list.

It would be a long and tedious business to repeat all the special rules for every unit within the army list itself. The army list is intended primarily as a tool for choosing armies rather than for presenting game rules. Wherever possible we have indicated where special rules apply and, where space permits, we have provided notes within the list as 'memory joggers'. Bear in mind that these descriptions are not necessarily exhaustive or definitive and players should refer to the main rules for a full account.

Dogs of War

Dogs of War are troops of other races who are prepared to fight under your flag in return for money, food, or some other suitable reward. A selection of such regiments are available as part of the Dogs of War range of models. The option to include Dogs of War units is included in the army list as part of the Rare Troops section.

Some players prefer to play without Dogs of War – choosing to field armies of pure and noble purpose unsullied by grubby financial transactions. If both players prefer to field armies without Dogs of War, they are free to agree beforehand not to employ untrustworthy sell-swords.

Conversely, if players wish to add more colour and variety to their armies then they may wish to employ more of these spectacular units. If both players agree beforehand, Dogs of War units can be included as Special unit choices as well as Rare ones.

LORDS

Lords (Highborn or High Sorceresses) are the most powerful and feared individuals in Naggaroth (after Malekith himself, of course).

Lords are severely limited in number (see page 25) and are quite expensive, but make the best army generals.

CHARACTERS' MOUNTS

Here are the profiles for mounts that can be ridden by Dark Elf characters. Full rules for these creatures can be found on pages 12-15.

	M	WS	BS	S	T	W	I	A	Ld
Dark Steed	9	3	0	3	3	1	4	1	5
Cold One	7	3	0	4	4	1	3	1	3
Dark Pegasus	8	3	0	4	4	3	4	2	6
Manticore	6	5	0	5	5	4	5	4	5
Black Dragon	6	6	0	6	6	6	3	5	8

Black Dragons are rare and powerful creatures, and a Lord on such a mount uses up an additional Hero slot in your army. For example, a Dark Elf Highborn on a Black Dragon is one Lord choice and one Hero choice.

DARK ELF HIGHBORN — Points/model: 125

	M	WS	BS	S	T	W	I	A	Ld
Highborn	5	7	6	4	3	3	8	4	10

Weapons: Hand weapon.

Options:
- May choose either an additional hand weapon (+6 pts), halberd (+6 pts), great weapon (+6 pts) or, if mounted, a lance (+6 pts).
- May also be armed with a repeater crossbow (+15 pts).
- May wear either light armour (+3 pts) or heavy armour (+6 pts), may be given a Sea Dragon cloak (+9 pts), and may also carry a shield (+3 pts).
- May ride either a Cold One (+39 pts), a Dark Steed (+18 pts), a Dark Pegasus (+55 pts), a Manticore (+190 pts), or a Black Dragon (+320 pts). Alternatively, may be mounted in a Cold One Chariot included as a separate Special choice, replacing one of the crew.
- May choose magic items from the Common or Dark Elf magic items lists, with a maximum total value of 100 points.

Special Rules:
  Hate High Elves.

HIGH SORCERESS — Points/model: 215

	M	WS	BS	S	T	W	I	A	Ld
High Sorceress	5	4	4	3	3	3	5	1	9

Weapons: Hand weapon.

Magic: A High Sorceress is a Level 3 Wizard. She may choose one of the following Lores: Shadow, Death or Dark Magic.

Options:
- May be upgraded to a Level 4 Wizard for +40 pts.
- May ride either a Dark Steed (+18 pts), a Cold One (+39 pts), a Dark Pegasus (+55 pts) or a Manticore (+190 pts).
- May choose magic items from the Common or Dark Elf magic items lists, with a maximum total value of 100 points.

Special Rules:
  Hate High Elves; Sect Enmity.

DARK ELF NOBLE*   Points/model: 70

	M	WS	BS	S	T	W	I	A	Ld
Noble	5	6	6	4	3	2	7	3	9

Weapons: Hand weapon.

Options:
- May choose an additional hand weapon (+4 pts), great weapon (+4 pts), halberd (+4 pts), or a lance if mounted (+4 pts).
- May also have a repeater crossbow (+10 pts).
- May wear either light armour (+2 pts) or heavy armour (+4 pts), may be given a Sea Dragon cloak (+6 pts), and may also carry a shield (+2 pts).
- May ride either a Dark Steed (+12 pts), Cold One (+26 pts), or a Dark Pegasus (+55 pts). Alternatively, he can be mounted in a Cold One Chariot included as a special choice, replacing one of the crew.
- May choose magic items from the Common or Dark Elf magic items lists, with a maximum total value of 50 pts.

Special Rules:
   Hate High Elves.

SORCERESS   Points/model: 90

	M	WS	BS	S	T	W	I	A	Ld
Sorceress	5	4	4	3	3	2	5	1	8

Weapons: Hand weapon.

Magic: A Sorceress is a Level 1 Wizard. She may choose one of the following Lores: Shadow, Death or Dark Magic.

Options:
- May be upgraded to a Level 2 Wizard for +40 pts.
- May ride a Dark Steed (+12 pts), or a Cold One (+26 pts).
- May choose magic items from the Common or Dark Elf magic items lists, with a maximum total value of 50 pts.

Special Rules:
   Hate High Elves; Sect Enmity.

BEASTMASTER**   Points/model: 40

	M	WS	BS	S	T	W	I	A	Ld
Beastmaster	5	4	4	3	3	2	6	2	8

Weapons: Whip (hand weapon).

Options:
- May choose an additional hand weapon (+4 pts).
- May ride either a a Dark Pegasus (+55 pts), a Cold One (+26 pts) or a Manticore (+190 pts).
- May choose magic items from the Common or Dark Elf magic items lists, with a maximum total value of 25 pts.

Special Rules:
   Hate High Elves; Beastmaster.

ASSASSIN   Points/model: 125

	M	WS	BS	S	T	W	I	A	Ld
Assassin	6	9	9	4	3	2	10	3	10

Weapons: Hand weapon.

Options:
- May choose an additional hand weapon (+4 pts).
- May choose magic items (with the exception of magic armour) or upgrades from the Temple of Khaine list (see pages 22-23), with a maximum total value of 50 pts.

Special Rules:
   Hate High Elves; Hidden; Leadership.

HEROES

Dark Elf Heroes are powerful characters with a variety of skills, such as the magic-wielding Sorceress or the deadly Assassin. Some Nobles have specific titles, such as the Captain of the Black Guard or the High Executioner.

The total number of characters you can field in your army can be found on page 25.

*BATTLE STANDARD BEARER
One Noble in the army may carry the Battle Standard for +25 pts.

The Battle Standard Bearer cannot be the army's General even if he has the highest Leadership value in the army.

The Battle Standard Bearer cannot be given any non-magical equipment except for light or heavy armour and a Sea Dragon cloak, or be mounted on a Dark Pegasus.

The Battle Standard Bearer can have any magic banner (no points limit), but if he carries a magic banner he cannot carry any other magic items.

**A Beastmaster mounted on a Manticore counts as two Hero choices.

CORE UNITS

Core units are the most common warriors in the army. There is a minimum number of Core units that must be fielded, and this varies with the size of the army (see page 25).

There is no maximum limit on the number of Core units that can be fielded.

DARK ELF WARRIORS — Points/model: 9

	M	WS	BS	S	T	W	I	A	Ld
Warrior	5	4	4	3	3	1	5	1	8
Lordling	5	4	4	3	3	1	5	2	8

Unit Size: 10+.

Weapons and Armour: Hand weapon, spear, light armour.

Options:
- Any unit may be equipped with shields for +1 pt/model.
- Any unit may replace spears with repeater crossbows for +4 pts/model.
- Upgrade one Warrior to a Musician for +5 pts.
- Upgrade one Warrior to a Standard Bearer for +10 pts.
- Promote one Warrior to a Lordling for +10 pts.

Special Rules:
 Hate High Elves.

CORSAIRS — Points/model: 10

	M	WS	BS	S	T	W	I	A	Ld
Corsair	5	4	4	3	3	1	5	1	8
Reaver	5	4	4	3	3	1	5	2	8

Unit Size: 10+

Weapons and Armour: Two hand weapons, light armour and Sea Dragon cloak.

Options:
- Upgrade one Corsair to a Musician for +5 pts.
- Upgrade one Corsair to a Standard Bearer for +10 pts.
- Promote one Corsair to a Reaver for +10 pts.
- One Corsair unit in the army may have a magic standard worth up to 50 points.

Special Rules:
 Hate High Elves.

DARK RIDERS — Points/model: 18

	M	WS	BS	S	T	W	I	A	Ld
Dark Rider	5	4	4	3	3	1	5	1	8
Herald	5	4	5	3	3	1	5	1	8
Dark Steed	9	3	0	3	3	1	4	1	5

Unit Size: 5+

Weapons and Armour: Hand weapon, light armour, spear.

Mounts: Dark Steed.

Options:
- Any unit may have repeater crossbows for +6 pts/model.
- Upgrade one Dark Rider to a Musician for +7 pts.
- Upgrade one Dark Rider to a Standard Bearer for +14 pts.
- Promote one Dark Rider to a Herald for +14 pts.

Special Rules:
 Riders *Hate* High Elves; Fast Cavalry.

SHADES

Points/model: 14

	M	WS	BS	S	T	W	I	A	Ld
Shade	5	4	4	3	3	1	5	1	8
Bloodshade	5	4	5	3	3	1	5	1	8

Unit Size: 5+

Weapons: Hand weapon and repeater crossbow.

Options:
- Any unit may have light armour for 1 pt/model.
- Promote one Shade to be a Bloodshade for +12 pts.

Special Rules:
Hate High Elves; Skirmishers; Scouts.

WITCH ELVES OF KHAINE

Points/model: 13

	M	WS	BS	S	T	W	I	A	Ld
Witch Elf	5	5	4	3	3	1	6	1	8
Hag	5	5	4	3	3	1	6	2	8

Unit Size: 10+.

Weapons: Two poisoned hand weapons.

Options:
- Upgrade one Witch Elf to a Musician for +6 pts.
- Upgrade one Witch Elf to a Standard Bearer for +12 pts.
- A Standard Bearer may carry a Magic Standard worth up to 50 pts.
- Promote one Witch Elf to a Hag for +12 pts.
- The Hag may have up to 25 points of items from the Temple of Khaine.

Special Rules:
Hate High Elves; Poisoned attacks; Devotees of Khaine; *Frenzy*.

COLD ONE CHARIOT

Points/model: 95

	M	WS	BS	S	T	W	I	A	Ld
Chariot	–	–	–	5	5	4	–	–	–
Crew	–	4	4	3	–	–	5	1	8
Cold One	7	3	–	4	–	–	3	1	–

Unit Size: Each Cold One Chariot is a separate unit, with two crew pulled by two Cold Ones.

Weapons: Crew carry hand weapons. The chariot has scythed wheels.

Armour Save: 4+

Options:
- The crew may have repeater crossbows for +10 pts and/or spears for +2 pts.
- Certain characters may ride in a chariot. They replace one of the crew, and the points value of the crew member is lost.

Special Rules:
Crew *Hate* High Elves; *Stupidity*; *Fear*; Chariot.

SPECIAL UNITS

There is a maximum number of Special units that can be fielded, and this varies with the size of the army (see page 25).

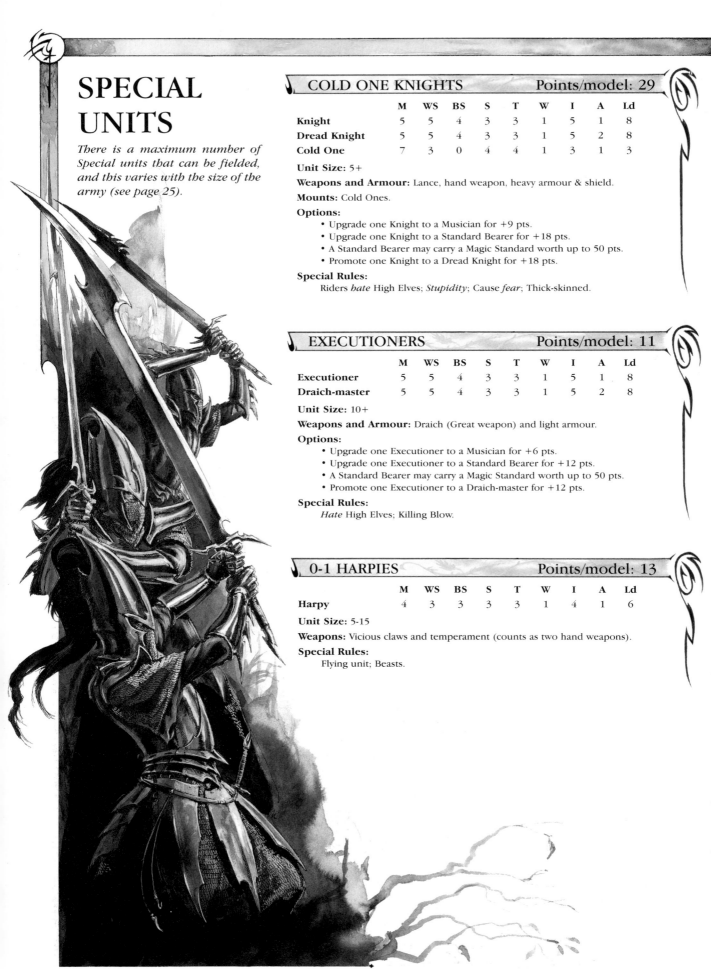

SPECIAL UNITS

There is a maximum number of Special units that can be fielded, and this varies with the size of the army (see page 25).

(see page 25)

COLD ONE KNIGHTS — Points/model: 29

	M	WS	BS	S	T	W	I	A	Ld
Knight	5	5	4	3	3	1	5	1	8
Dread Knight	5	5	4	3	3	1	5	2	8
Cold One	7	3	0	4	4	1	3	1	3

Unit Size: 5+

Weapons and Armour: Lance, hand weapon, heavy armour & shield.

Mounts: Cold Ones.

Options:
- Upgrade one Knight to a Musician for +9 pts.
- Upgrade one Knight to a Standard Bearer for +18 pts.
- A Standard Bearer may carry a Magic Standard worth up to 50 pts.
- Promote one Knight to a Dread Knight for +18 pts.

Special Rules:
Riders *hate* High Elves; *Stupidity*; Cause *fear*; Thick-skinned.

EXECUTIONERS — Points/model: 11

	M	WS	BS	S	T	W	I	A	Ld
Executioner	5	5	4	3	3	1	5	1	8
Draich-master	5	5	4	3	3	1	5	2	8

Unit Size: 10+

Weapons and Armour: Draich (Great weapon) and light armour.

Options:
- Upgrade one Executioner to a Musician for +6 pts.
- Upgrade one Executioner to a Standard Bearer for +12 pts.
- A Standard Bearer may carry a Magic Standard worth up to 50 pts.
- Promote one Executioner to a Draich-master for +12 pts.

Special Rules:
Hate High Elves; Killing Blow.

0-1 HARPIES — Points/model: 13

	M	WS	BS	S	T	W	I	A	Ld
Harpy	4	3	3	3	3	1	4	1	6

Unit Size: 5-15

Weapons: Vicious claws and temperament (counts as two hand weapons).

Special Rules:
Flying unit; Beasts.

WAR HYDRA — Points/model: 220

	M	WS	BS	S	T	W	I	A	Ld
War Hydra	6	4	0	5	5	6	2	5	6
Apprentice	5	4	4	3	3	1	5	1	8

Unit Size: One War Hydra, driven into battle by two Beastmaster Apprentices.

Weapons: Apprentices have two hand weapons.

Special Rules:

Breathe Fire; *Terror*; Controlled; Large creature; Scaly Skin.
Apprentices *hate* High Elves.

0-1 BLACK GUARD — Points/model: 16

	M	WS	BS	S	T	W	I	A	Ld
Black Guard	5	5	4	3	3	1	6	1	9
Master	5	5	4	3	3	1	6	2	9

Unit Size: 10+

Weapons and Armour: Halberd, heavy armour.

Options:
- Upgrade one Black Guard to a Musician for +7 pts.
- Upgrade one Black Guard to a Standard Bearer for +14 pts.
- A Standard Bearer may carry a Magic Standard worth up to 75 pts.
- Promote one Black Guard to a Master for +14 pts.

Special Rules:

Hatred; *Stubborn*.

RARE UNITS

There is a maximum number of Rare units that can be fielded, and this varies with the size of the army (see page 25).

Amongst the most devastating units are the Witch King's personal troops – the deadly and vicious Black Guard of Naggarond.

An army can have a maximum of **one** *unit of Black Guard.*

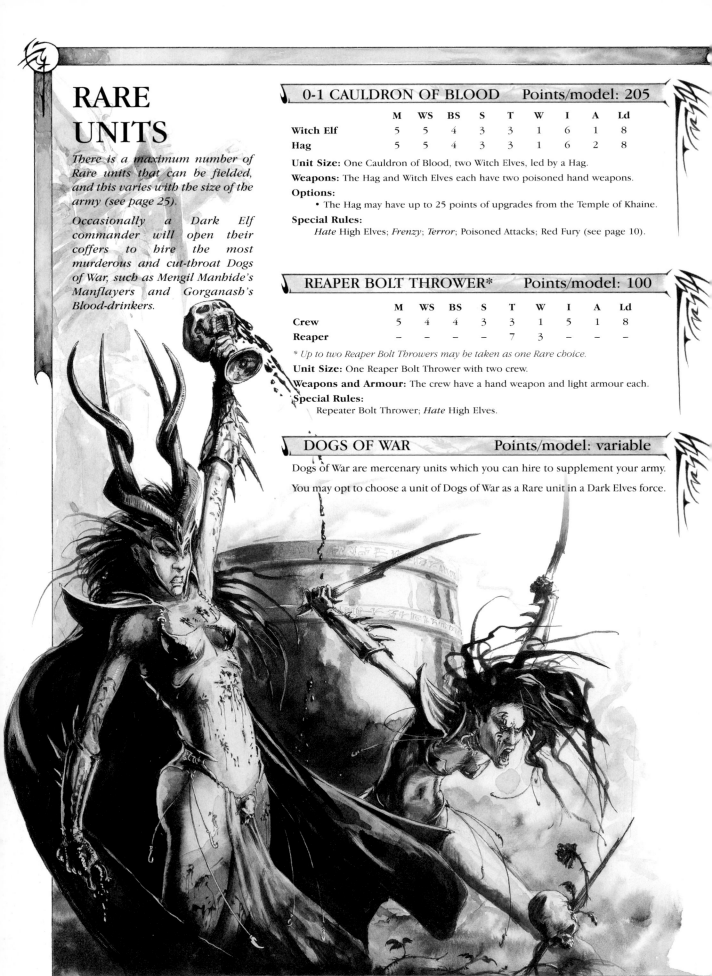

RARE UNITS

There is a maximum number of Rare units that can be fielded, and this varies with the size of the army (see page 25).

Occasionally a Dark Elf commander will open their coffers to hire the most murderous and cut-throat Dogs of War, such as Mengil Manhide's Manflayers and Gorganash's Blood-drinkers.

0-1 CAULDRON OF BLOOD   Points/model: 205

	M	WS	BS	S	T	W	I	A	Ld
Witch Elf	5	5	4	3	3	1	6	1	8
Hag	5	5	4	3	3	1	6	2	8

Unit Size: One Cauldron of Blood, two Witch Elves, led by a Hag.

Weapons: The Hag and Witch Elves each have two poisoned hand weapons.

Options:
  • The Hag may have up to 25 points of upgrades from the Temple of Khaine.

Special Rules:
  Hate High Elves; *Frenzy*; *Terror*; Poisoned Attacks; Red Fury (see page 10).

REAPER BOLT THROWER*   Points/model: 100

	M	WS	BS	S	T	W	I	A	Ld
Crew	5	4	4	3	3	1	5	1	8
Reaper	–	–	–	–	7	3	–	–	–

* Up to two Reaper Bolt Throwers may be taken as one Rare choice.

Unit Size: One Reaper Bolt Thrower with two crew.

Weapons and Armour: The crew have a hand weapon and light armour each.

Special Rules:
  Repeater Bolt Thrower; *Hate* High Elves.

DOGS OF WAR   Points/model: variable

Dogs of War are mercenary units which you can hire to supplement your army.

You may opt to choose a unit of Dogs of War as a Rare unit in a Dark Elves force.

PAINTING A DARK ELF ARMY

A fully painted army arrayed for battle is an impressive sight. For many people it is the inspiration which sparks the desire to collect their own force. The mere thought of painting a whole army may seem a little daunting at first. Don't worry though, you'd be surprised at how quickly your new army takes shape and how enjoyable the whole process actually becomes. Make no mistake, an army doesn't appear overnight, and it requires patience. However, the reward gained from owning and playing with a beautifully painted army makes all the effort more than worthwhile.

If you are a newcomer to Warhammer don't worry too much about the quality of your painting. Many of the figures shown on the following pages are painted by the highly skilled 'Eavy Metal team. These talented guys and gals spend every day of the week painting figures, and achieve standards that even those of us who have been painting for quite some time can only dream of matching. Whilst few of us will ever own a force painted to such an extraordinarily high quality, this doesn't mean that we can't all aim to come close or even to better our standards with each new figure we paint. With time and patience, one day you may even be the proud owner of a legendary Golden Demon award.

In this section of the book we will show you a variety of easy to learn techniques and tips with which to help you paint your figures. In a short time you will have developed the skills necessary to invent your own painting and modelling methods and chosen the colours for a truly unique army.

It is important to remember that there is no correct way to paint your army. Time and patience are the key elements to increase a small raiding force into a sizeable Dark Elf army. We hope the models on the following page inspire you to create your own uniquely painted models. Try experimenting with the various techniques until you find the one that suits you. If getting your army straight into battle is more important to you then choose a quick method. If you'd rather take your time painting an army that will make your friends drool with envy, then use the more detailed techniques to paint your models.

More than anything the models on the following pages are there to inform and inspire. We hope that this section of the book lends you an insight into the wonderfully diverse world of painting. As your army grows you will find that your skills also improve, and before too long you may even be collecting your second or third army. Most importantly we hope that you have fun.

PAINTING DARK ELVES

Dark Elf warriors form the backbone of your army. Once you've mastered some simple techniques for painting chainmail and plate armour you'll soon have your regiments of Spearmen and Crossbowmen ready for battle.

Before you begin to paint your models you should take into consideration how you want your army to look once it is complete. Dark Elves are an evil, cruel race and a dark, menacing colour scheme really captures this spirit.

A few well chosen colours will have more of an impact than lots of different ones, so a good start is to select a limited palette of paints to use. Your army will probably feature quite a lot of Chaos Black, which can be complimented by dark tones such as Liche Purple or Dark Angels Green. In contrast, bright, polished armour using Chainmail and/or Shining Gold provides some relief from all the dark colours, as does a pale skin tone.

As your Spearmen and Crossbowmen are modelled wearing lots of armour, we recommend undercoating them with Chaos Black as this produces a better result for painting armour. Chainmail, Mithril Silver or Shining Gold can be used to paint the armour of your Dark Elves. Of course you are not limited to painting in metallic colours. You can experiment with various colours to give the impression that the armour is covered in dark lacquer. However, to give a unit a coherent look it's best to use the same armour technique on all the models.

The final stage is to base your figure. Whether you choose to use flock, static grass or sand, you should use the same technique on each model in the army. This will give the whole force a really cohesive appearance.

This Crossbowman's armour has been drybrushed using Chainmail.

Here the breastplates and helmet have been painted Shining Gold. Gold trim has been added to the hem of the chainmail.

This Spearman's plate armour has been painted Chaos Black and highlighted Jade Green.

Games Workshop's website (www.games-workshop.com) has plenty of painting and modelling ideas. On it you will find a hobby guide which gives great tips on a variety of painting techniques. The site also links to other independent sites which you may find useful.

Here we have chosen a Liche Purple colour scheme to paint the hems and sleeves of the robes. This gives the models a more unified appearance when put together as a regiment. Note the contrast between the pale flesh tones against the darker colours of the armour and clothing.

Drybrushing is a simple and effective method to quickly paint textured surfaces. Dip your brush in the chosen colour then wipe most of the paint away on a paper towel. By dragging your brush lightly across the model a small amount of paint will adhere to the surface of the miniature, picking out the texture. This method is very effective for painting chainmail and will allow you to paint your force quickly.

In the case of Spearmen models the shield forms a prominent part of the figure and is easy to paint. Select a background colour which complements the colour scheme of your regiment. You can unify the regiment by using the same shield icon on each model. You could even continue with the same design across the whole army.

The troops in the Witch King's Invasion Force have the shield icons of their regiments painted onto their banner as a common motif.

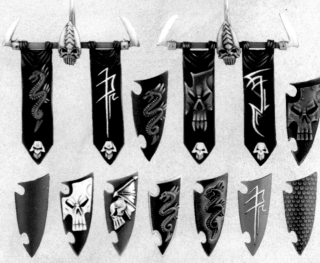

You can paint shields simply with a single flat colour or add an icon painted metal or a contrasting colour. You may find it easier to paint the icons on their frame before fixing them to the shields. For elite units and character models you can be more elaborate, adding borders, colourful backgrounds and intricate shield designs.

LORD YEURL'S MIDNIGHT RAIDERS
BY DAVID GALLAGHER

Dave is one of Games Workshop's veteran artists and is responsible for all of the artwork within this book. As you can imagine this leaves him little time to paint miniatures, so Dave needed to find a fast method to complete his army.

"The basic undercoat of Chaos Black has been highlighted with Gloss Varnish for a great effect. I wanted to achieve an archaic but varied feel to the entire force so used a number of different colours to paint the armour of each of my regiments. Coupled with Midnight Blue for the cloth and static grass for the bases the overall effect is a quickly painted but striking army."

● Chaos Black/ Gloss Varnish

● Blood Red/ Red ink

○ Shining Gold

ASSEMBLING DARK ELF REGIMENTS

Before you start painting your regiments, it's worthwhile giving some thought as to how your models will fit together. Models which 'rank up' will look a lot better once they are on the battlefield.

Before you begin the process of painting your models you'll need to assemble them. It is all too easy to forget that models have to rank up into a unit. Try assembling one rank at a time; stand the models next to each other loose on their bases to see how they fit before finally gluing them on. This way you can be sure they will rank up. An effective method of making certain that the models fit neatly into ranks is to glue them onto regimental bases which carry four models.

You should try to position the crossbows of your rear rankers either pointing downward or facing up so that they can rank up behind the front models.

Spear-armed units look better if you have the front rank with their spears pointing forwards and the rest angled up. You could even position the second rank poking their spears over the heads of the front rankers.

PAINTING KORHEDRON'S REAVERS BY MATTHEW HUTSON

1   2   3   4   5

Matthew Hutson is a member of Games Workshop's White Dwarf team. He has been painting Dark Elves for over six years and this is the second Dark Elf army he has collected.

Matt: *For my Dark Elf army I decided to go for a simple colour scheme that was based on only two colours, red and black. Here's how I painted my Dark Elf Warriors:* **1)** *I started by spraying them black and then drybrushed the metal areas with Boltgun Metal. It's very difficult to be neat with drybrushing so I tidied up the black areas with Chaos Black.* **2)** *Next, I painted all the armoured areas with a mixture of Blood Red and Chaos Black. When this was dry I painted the skin with Vomit Brown and highlighted the black areas using Codex Grey.* **3)** *At this point I gave the skin areas a coat of Flesh Wash and highlighted the armoured areas by painting Blood Red on all the edges.* **4)** *Making sure the Flesh Wash had dried I next highlighted the skin with Bleached Bone before giving the armour its last highlight using Vomit Brown.* **5)** *To finish off my Warriors I gave their armour a Red Glaze to bring together all the highlights before basing the model and attaching the shields.*

KORHEDRON'S REAVERS

The red and black colour scheme Matt chose runs throughout every part of his force. Each of his Cold Ones has been painted in the same tone of green and he's used a common banner design. All these elements, combined with a consistent basing technique, makes for a neat and cohesive army.

Dark Elf Warriors with repeater crossbows

Lord Korhedron mounted on a Cold One

Assassin

Corsair regiment

DARK ELF REGIMENTS

When painting a Dark Elf army its better to consider it in terms of whole regiments rather than being made up of individual models. The colours you use will dictate the overall look of your army.

The bulk of a Dark Elf army consists of Spearmen and Crossbowmen. Consistent use of your limited pallette throughout your units will make them look like a single army rather than a random mass of fighters. You may even wish to continue with this colour scheme by carrying it through to your banners and war machines wherever possible. Of course you may prefer to paint individual regiments with different colours. This will help you to pick them out from each other on the battlefield. You may also want to use different shield and banner designs to do this. Whether you do them all the same, or vary your units, you should stick with this method throughout the army.

Corsair Champion

Corsair Champion

The Sea Dragon cloaks of the Corsairs give you the opportunity to add a little colour variation to your force. This unit's cloaks have been painted using Scaly Green, highlighted with Jade Green, with Scorched Brown highlighted with Bronzed Flesh for the leathery underside.

You can see above how we have used the theme of a white rune on the banners to visually link all of our warrior regiments.

As their name would suggest Dark Riders wear a great deal of black. You are not limited to this colour alone, the harnesses of the horses and the bandanas of the riders can be painted to fit the colours of your army.

It is a good idea to paint the riders and steeds separately and fix them together afterwards. This way, you will find it easier to paint the areas which would otherwise be obscured or difficult to reach with a paintbrush.

Dark Rider with repeater crossbow

For our Warrior units we have painted the shafts of the crossbows and the standard pole with Bestial Brown. You could use any colour to paint these parts but you may find it best to stick to neutral tones so as not to distract from your main colour scheme.

ELITE REGIMENTS

These regiments form specialised units on the battlefield, and as such you will probably want them to stand out from the bulk of your force. They provide the ideal opportunity to add some variety and colour.

Unlike most other Dark Elf regiments there is a large area of flesh to paint on the Witch Elf models. The 'Eavy Metal team have painted these Witch Elves with a very pale skin tone using a base coat of Elf flesh highlighted with Skull White.

Because units such as the Witch Elves, Har Ganeth Executioners and the Black Guard have a unique appearance, the addition of an extra colour or two to your limited palette is the simplest and most effective way to distinguish them as Elite units. This will have the effect of making the unit stand out from the basic regiments of Spearmen and Crossbowmen that make up most of your force. It is surprising how effective the addition of a single extra colour to a limited palette can achieve a varied appearance to your army.

-A small amount of Shining Gold has been added to the intricate armour of our Black Guard. This contrasts with the black robes to make the unit really stand out. Note how the common runic banner theme of the army is still used on this Rare unit.

Black Guard Champion

Because Shades strike at their foes from the shadows they need to be well camouflaged. Even the purple that ties them in as part of their army has been shaded in a darker tone.

Black Guard Musician

These Executioners of Har Ganeth are distinguished by the large amount of gold on their armour. This shows the unit to be a unique elite troop type. Only the smallest hint of purple signifies them as part of our Naggaroth force.

The pale flesh and dark wings and legs of the Harpies means that even this strange unit fits in with our army colour scheme.

COLD ONES

The heavily armoured Dark Elf Knights ride fearsome reptiles to battle. When thinking up a scheme for our Cold Ones, we took our inspiration from a variety of books on dinosaurs and reptiles.

Space Wolves Grey · Blood Red

Dark Flesh · Goblin Green

Vomit Brown · Scaly Green

Dark Angels Green · Red Gore

Vomit Brown · Chaos Black

Regal Blue · Ghostly Grey, Regal Blue mix

These Cold Ones have been painted with a base coat of Camo Green to give a natural reptilian look to the skin. The scales were then picked out using a mix of Camo Green and Chaos Black, with the addition of Bleached Bone to highlight the edges. Like our other elite regiments, use of gold on the Knights' armour marks them out from the Core regiments.

The Cold One Knights of our Army of the North have been painted using the colour scheme of Shining Gold armour used throughout the army. The Cold Ones have been painted using Midnight Blue as a base colour, which works well as a contrast colour against the gold and is in keeping with the rest of the force.

This Cold One Chariot is also part of our Army of the North and has the same colour scheme applied to it as the Cold One Knights.

SCALY SKIN

Cold Ones offer you the chance to add some extra colour to your army and there are a number of different methods to paint them. Using ink washes or drybrushing techniques you will quickly pick out the individual scales.

You can also paint the scales in a contrasting colour to the skin to make them stand out. Alternatively, you could leave them the same overall colour and paint a pattern over the top.

Inkwashing is a simple technique done by painting a darker tone of specially designed ink or watered down Citadel paints over the base colour of the model where it will settle into the crevices and create a shaded effect.

HYDRA

You may want to paint your War Hydra with its own colour scheme or use the same colours as your Cold Ones. Use your established colours on the Beastmaster Apprentices to visually link them with the rest of the army.

BEASTMASTER ON MANTICORE

The Manticore has been painted using natural colours such as Scorched Brown and Snakebite Leather. In contrast the robes of the rider have been painted with our Invasion Force colour scheme.

THE WITCH KING'S INVASION FORCE OF NAGGAROTH

As you can see the purple colour scheme which the 'Eavy Metal team has chosen unifies the whole army. By sticking to a few basic colours, the final result is very effective. With subtle variations in details, such as the icons on the banners, each unit can develop its own unique character whilst still retaining the overall colour scheme of the army.

TERRAIN

The perfect addition to a fully painted Dark Elf army is some specially themed terrain. It will not only add to the overall look of your army but make your battles far more spectacular.

Mark Jones tells us how he made the terrain piece shown above: "I wanted to make an offering pool where ritual sacrifices took place, including a large tree with bodies hung from it. The tree I found at a pet store and I cut a base for it from a piece of hardboard. I glued the tree down with superglue and then built up the bank for a pool from modelling clay. Once it was dry I added small rocks and sand to texture the top."

"Then I undercoated the whole model with Black spray and drybrushed it with Vermin Brown and Bubonic Brown. I drybrushed the bank with Codex Grey and Ghostly Grey, painting the skulls with Bestial Brown and Bleached Bone. The pool was painted Scaly Green and gloss varnished to look like water. I added static grass to blend the terrain with the rest that we'd made. The final touch was the skeletons hung from the tree after I'd finished painted it."

WAR MACHINES

A great centrepiece for the Dark Elf army is the huge Cauldron of Blood. It's worth spending some extra time and attention when painting this model as it will be a focal point of your army.

We have chosen to paint the statue of Khaine with a green marble effect to make it stand out from the rest of the army. The Witch Elf devotees have been painted in the army's purple colour scheme, and additional touches of Shining Gold have been added to the Hag Queen model to display her importance.

Cauldron of Blood and Reaper Bolt Throwers

MASTERS OF EVIL

For thousands of years the Dark Elves have ruled Naggaroth. In that time there have been many among their number who have risen to greatness – infamous across the world for their acts of depravity and skill at arms. They are the stuff of nightmares, their names told to small children across the Old World to get them to behave. They are the darker shadows in the night, the creatures that prey on the weak, the hunters who never tire.

On this page are a few of the greatest warriors of the Dark Elves. We hope that they will inspire you to greatness with your own army, and perhaps you can work out rules to include them in your games. On the following pages are rules for three of the most well known characters in Naggaroth – the Witch King himself, his mother Morathi the Hag Sorceress and Malus Darkblade, the daemon-possessed noble of Hag Graef. You may include any of these in your army as detailed in their individual descriptions.

You need not agree with your opponent beforehand if you wish to use Malekith, Morathi or Malus, but you should discuss using other special characters of your own devising with your opponent.

BEASTLORD RAKARTH OF KAROND KAR

Rakarth is the most accomplished beastmaster in the whole of Naggaroth. When Rakarth was just a child his father was attempting to break and train the mighty Black Dragon Bracchus.

However, the Dragon was more than a match for even his father's considerable skills and in a fit of rage the Dark Elf Beastmaster ordered the Dragon to be slain. Rakarth made a deal with his father to allow him to keep the monstrous beast if he could ride it, and his father duly agreed. Rakarth fixed the Dragon with his piercing stare, and there was something in the young Dark Elf that the Dragon recognised. Bracchus saw the innate cruelty and bloodlust of Rakarth, and knew that a kindred spirit approached. The Dragon acquiesced to Rakarth without a fight, and he has ridden Bracchus into battle ever since.

KOURAN, CAPTAIN OF THE BLACK GUARD

Kouran rose to his exalted position as the commander of Malekith's personal bodyguard with a mixture of cunning and ruthlessness. He cares nothing for the lives of other mortals, save the Witch King and Morathi, and has been known to sacrifice entire armies to defend the Dark Elf realm. All fear his wrath and, under his merciless leadership, the army of Naggarond has crushed every foe it has faced with him at its head.

TULLARIS OF HAR GANETH

As the leader of the rightly feared Executioners, it is Tullaris who is responsible for wreaking the Witch King's retribution on those who displease him. He is murderous and savage, delighting in the terror of others. He finds great pleasure in the exquisite moment between the accused lowering their head on the block and the kiss of the blade across their neck. It is claimed that he once butchered all the inhabitants of a town in the Empire, and razed the settlement to the ground, simply because its name irked him! Even the mere rumour of Tullaris leading a Dark Elf host is enough to cause floods of refugees to flee before his army.

SHADOWBLADE, MASTER OF ASSASSINS

Even though still young by Dark Elf standards (a mere 150 years old), Shadowblade is the greatest Assassin ever to be trained by the Temple of Khaine. He is a legend amongst the Druchii, his exploits told as fireside tales to eager Dark Elf children. Most celebrated of all is his single-handed massacre of the entire crew of a High Elf Hawkship, whom he murdered one by one over several days, each killed in a different fashion. The mere thought of Shadowblade's murderous attentions is enough to keep all but the most stupid or brave Dark Elf noble from plotting against the Witch King.

MALEKITH, WITCH KING OF NAGGAROTH

Malekith was the son of Aenarion, the first of the High Elf Phoenix Kings, and the mysterious and beautiful seeress Morathi. He grew to be a mighty warrior, a great sorcerer and a brilliant general. When Aenarion died, a brief time of peace followed and there were many Elves who believed that Malekith, a ruthless warrior who had proven himself in the harsh war-torn lands of Nagarythe, was unsuitable to take his father's place as king. Bel-Shannar was chosen to rule in his stead.

Malekith bitterly accepted their decision and took on the role of commander of the Ulthuan army. He proved to be a brilliant young general, for many decades gaining power and allies with his glorious victories. Then one dark winter he made his move to usurp the throne. Claiming that the Phoenix King was a follower of Chaos, he secretly assassinated him by means of an undetectable poison.

Believing the throne to be his by right, he stepped into the flames of Asuryan to prove himself worthy, but the flames would not accept his polluted body. Instead they engulfed his soul, casting him out and leaving his mortal body terribly scarred.

Morathi carried her injured son from the temple and nursed him back to health over many years. As Malekith gradually recovered he ordered that a suit of armour be forged and had it fused to his own withered body in order that it would lend him its magical strength. To the brow of the great horned helmet was welded the Circlet of Iron, a talisman of awesome sorcerous power. He set about waging a civil war and, although he was forced into exile after defeat within the lands of Ulthuan, he travelled west and discovered a new continent which he claimed for himself, naming the kingdom Naggaroth.

For over five thousand years he and his followers have continued to wage war against the Phoenix Kings. Countless numbers of Elves have been slain in the bitter civil war, and Malekith has come close to claiming the throne that is rightfully his many times. His last incursion into the land of Ulthuan was only repulsed after two years of relentless warfare. Now the Witch King has a new weapon with which to cast a shadow over the realm of the High Elves. Over thousands of years he has been secretly hoarding a clutch of Dragon eggs. Now the first of the hatchlings have matured. Trained by the skilled Beastmasters over a period of many centuries, the young Dragons have grown strong and are at last ready for battle. Malekith now rides Seraphon, the strongest of the first batch. His finest Knights have been tutored to ride these terrible beasts into battle, and with them Malekith plans to unleash a deadly assault upon the forces of Ulthuan.

	M	WS	BS	S	T	W	I	A	Ld
Malekith	5	8	5	4	3	3	8	4	10
Seraphon	6	6	0	6	6	6	4	5	8

Malekith is the ruler of all the Dark Elves. He can be taken as one of your Lord choices. In addition, he also uses up three of your Hero choices. This means that he will fill one Lord and three Hero choices in total. He must be used exactly as presented here and may not be given any additional equipment or magic items.

Points: 945

Weapons: Malekith wields Destroyer and the Hand of Khaine. These count as two hand weapons and so give him an extra Attack. He may divide his Attacks between each weapon freely; nominate how many he will make with each at the start of every combat round. He must allocate a minimum of one Attack to each weapon.

Armour: Malekith is protected by the Armour of Midnight.

Mount: Malekith rides the Black Dragon Seraphon into battle.

SPECIAL RULES

Sorcerer

Malekith is highly skilled at the Dark Arts and so is a Fourth Level Wizard. He will always use Dark Magic.

Black Guard

Malekith's personal bodyguards are the Black Guard of Naggarond. If your army is led by Malekith, Black Guard are no longer a 0-1 choice – you may include as many units as you have Rare choices.

Burning Hatred

Such is Malekith's hatred of the High Elves, he may re-roll missed close combat attacks against them in any round of combat, not just the first round.

Absolute Power

Malekith is the unchallenged ruler of all the Dark Elves and all bow to his authority. If you include Malekith in your army he must be the army general.

MAGIC ITEMS

Destroyer

Malekith's blade was forged in ancient Ulthuan and enchanted to destroy other magical items.

If Malekith hits an opponent with a magic weapon or with magic armour, instead of rolling to wound you may choose to destroy one item (opponent's choice). He may only destroy one item in each round of combat. Resolve this before making any rolls to wound or attacks with the Hand of Khaine.

Hand of Khaine

Malekith's armour incorporates the Hand of Khaine, a magical gauntlet which can tear off limbs and crush the skulls of his foes.

Any attacks Malekith makes with the Hand of Khaine are resolved at Strength 6, and ignore armour saves.

Armour of Midnight

Forged from the hardest meteoric iron to be mined from the mountains of Naggaroth, Malekith's armour is near impenetrable to mortal weapons.

The Armour of Midnight is a suit of heavy armour. In addition Malekith has a 2+ Ward save against any non-magical attacks (ie, not spells or magic items). Also, he will never suffer more than one wound from a single hit, so war machines, magic items and other attacks that cause multiple wounds only ever cause one wound at a time. The Armour of Midnight does not prevent Malekith from casting spells.

MORATHI, THE HAG SORCERESS

After the Witch King himself, Morathi is the most powerful Dark Elf in all of Naggaroth. Born to scheming and politics, and a talented Sorceress, Morathi has spent five thousand years teaching her son all she knows of statecraft and magic, and works to maintain his grip on the throne of Naggaroth.

Morathi has always had the taint of Chaos about her – she met Malekith's father, Aenarion the first Phoenix King, when the Elven lord rescued her from a Chaos warband. It is believed that it was during her time as a captive that Chaos first crept into her soul. It was Morathi who started the Cult of Pleasure on Ulthuan, which eventually led to the bloody civil war of the Sundering. Morathi also first perfected the Dark Art, opening up gateways to the Chaos hells to receive unimaginable powers. Combined with her beauty and intellect, it is Morathi's magical abilities which allow her to hold sway over her enemies.

Morathi is the first Hag Queen of the Witch Elves, and although the sect now follows her rival, Hellebron, many who worship at the Temple of Khaine owe loyalty to the Sorceress. It is also claimed that Morathi brought forth the first Cauldron of Blood, some say given to her by bloodthirsty Khaine himself. Once a year, on Death Night, she bathes in the boiling blood within the cauldron, rejuvenating her old, tired flesh and emerging from the steam as young and beautiful as the day she left the shores of Ulthuan. No other Hag Queen has lived as long as Morathi, and Hellebron, forbidden access to the true Cauldron of Blood, withers and ages with every passing year. It is a source of much bitterness between them.

It is Morathi and Morathi alone of the Witch Elves who is allowed to wield magical power; like her son, Morathi feels no shame in creating laws and traditions for the control of others, whilst ignoring them herself. Over the millennia, Morathi has struck daemonic pacts with many vile and disturbing forces, and can unleash the power of Chaos with a thought. She is capable of the most powerful magics possible, and some believe it was her plan to destroy Ulthuan's magical vortex and unleash the hells of Chaos upon the world.

Morathi is totally dedicated to her son, as he is to her, and though some would say their relationship is unnatural, between them they rule Naggaroth with an iron grip and bloodied sword.

	M	WS	BS	S	T	W	I	A	Ld
Morathi	5	5	4	4	3	3	6	3	10
Sulephet	8	3	0	4	4	3	4	2	6

Morathi is the mother of the Witch King and second only to him in power. She can be taken as one of your Lord choices. She must be used exactly as presented here and may not be given any additional equipment or magic items.

Points: 470

Weapons: Morathi wields Heartrender.

Armour: Morathi is protected by the Thousand and One Dark Blessings.

Mount: Morathi rides her Dark Pegasus Sulephet.

MAGIC ITEMS

Heartrender

Such is Morathi's skill with the lance-like Heartrender she can pluck a victim's heart from their chest with a single well-placed blow.

On the turn Morathi charges, Heartrender adds +2 to her Strength. In addition, when she is charging she gains the Killing Blow special rule.

SPECIAL RULES

High Sorceress

Morathi is a Fourth Level Dark Elf Sorceress. She always uses Dark Magic, but you may choose which four spells she has at the start of the battle, rather than rolling for them. In addition, Morathi adds +2 to all of her casting rolls, rather than the normal +1.

Beloved of Khaine

Morathi is the first of the Hag Queens, and all Witch Elves owe allegiance to her before any other. Any Witch Elves within 12" of Morathi may use her Leadership value, as if she was their army General. If Morathi is in your army Witch Elves may not use the army General's Leadership.

Thousand and One Dark Blessings

Morathi has ancients pacts with many malevolent spirits and daemonic entities, whose unnatural energies protect her from harm. This has the effect of giving her a 4+ Ward save and Magic Resistance (1).

Enchanting Beauty

Morathi is possibly the most beautiful woman in the known world, and mere mortals are enraptured by her. Any enemy model in base contact with Morathi at the start of a round of combat must pass a Leadership test or have their WS reduced to 1 for the duration of that round.

MALUS DARKBLADE, SCION OF HAG GRAEF

The tale of Malus Darkblade is one of greed, treachery and much bloodshed. Born of one of the noble families of Hag Graef, Malus was the pride of his father – ruthless, bloodthirsty, cunning and ambitious. To further his own political power, Malus sought out an ancient magical treasure but, in discovering it, he also found something much older and more terrible.

Malus was possessed by the daemon Tz'arkan, his life and soul were forfeit. He had but one way of escaping his fate – to find five unholy artifacts of power which could be used in the ritual to free Tz'arkan for eternity and restore Malus' soul. He had but a year and day to succeed. Long and hard was his quest for the five treasures, and many were his battles along the way. Many foes fell beneath his blade; foul Minotaurs, Orcs and a mighty Dragon Ogre lie dead in his wake. Such was Malus' determination and ruthlessness that he slew his own father for possession of the Dagger of Torxus, one of the artifacts needed for his salvation. For this, the Dark Elf bards also call Malus the Kinslayer.

Upon the eve of his doom, Malus returned to the place of his possession and performed the ritual, but Tz'arkan had tricked the Dark Elf lord. Upon escaping from Malus' body, the treacherous daemon took his soul as well, and thus Darkblade became known as the Soulless One. Caught between life and death, Malus wandered the Chaos Wastes for a decade, fighting and killing for others. He cared not whether he lived or died and so fought in battle like no mortal creature. Armed with the Warpsword of Khaine, the only artefact not destroyed in the ritual to free himself, Malus was unstoppable and, though he craved death, there was none skilled or strong enough to defeat him.

It was during this time that Malus learned of the new lair of Tz'arkan from a sorcerer. The magic user knew of Darkblade's treacherous nature and hoped to forestall any betrayal by having the map tattooed to his back. Malus cared not, and flayed the map from the sorcerer, feeding the rest to his Cold One,

Spite. Once more Malus travelled many leagues and fought against many creatures of the Four Powers and his own enemies from Naggaroth before locating the daemon who had stolen his soul.

Unfortunately for Malus, the resting place of Tz'arkan was within the realm of the Screaming God-Child, a twisted being sworn to Chaos Undivided; a hell place at the heart of the Realms of Chaos from which it was claimed that no mortal could pass back. But Malus, the master of cunning, tricked the Screaming God-Child and managed to escape. Upon realising the devious Malus had eluded him, the Screaming God-Child cursed the Dark Elf, and as punishment once more imprisoned Tz'arkan within him.

Now, after many years of journeying, Malus has returned to Hag Graef. None know his true intentions, but he has lost none of his thirst for power.

MALUS DARKBLADE

	M	WS	BS	S	T	W	I	A	Ld
Malus	5	7	5	4	3	3	8	4	10
Spite	7	3	0	4	4	1	3	2	3

Malus is a Dark Elf Noble who has recently returned from many adventures in the Chaos Wastes. He can be taken as one of your Lord choices. In addition, he also uses up a Hero choice. This means that he will fill one Lord and one Hero choice in total. He must be used exactly as presented here and may not be given any additional equipment or magic items.

Points: 350

Weapons: Malus wields the Warpsword of Khaine.

Armour: Malus wears heavy armour. Combined with his Cold One mount, this gives him a 3+ armour save.

Mount: Malus rides his Cold One, Spite. Unlike other Cold Ones, Spite does not suffer from *Stupidity*.

MAGIC ITEMS

Warpsword of Khaine

This is one of the five fabled treasures that Malus had to retrieve in his quest to rid himself of the daemon that possesses him.

The Warpsword of Khaine ignores armour saves. In addition, Malus may re-roll any failed rolls to wound when wielding the Warpsword.

SPECIAL RULES

Tz'Arkan

Malus succumbs to Tz'arkan's possession when asleep, and drinks a magical potion to keep himself awake. When he needs the power of the daemon, he imbibes a dark elixir which immediately causes him to lose consciousness, allowing Tz'arkan to take control.

At the start of any Dark Elf turn, Malus may drink his soporific potion and unleash the power of the daemon that resides within him. If he does this, it has the following effects that last for the remainder of the battle:

Malus is subject to *frenzy* and does not lose his frenzy even if beaten in combat.

Malus adds +1WS, +1S, +2T and +2I.

He may re-roll any failed Leadership test he is required to take (for spells, Break tests, etc).

If Malus is in base contact with a friendly model and not in contact with the enemy in any Close Combat phase (including your opponent's) roll a D6. On a roll of a 4+ he restrains his murderous rage. On a 3 or less he attacks one model in contact chosen by your opponent, resolved as if he was charging, The other model will strike back if it survives Malus' attacks. No combat results are calculated and both models will act normally from the moment the attacks are finished.

THE SLAVE'S TALE

My name is Hargan, my second name is of little consequence.

Once I felt the tenderness and love of a warm, caring family, but they are gone. Whether they still live or not is of no importance, for emotion is a luxury that has long since been lost to me.

Once, in what seems like another lifetime, I remember I was scribe to the Burgomeister of Marienburg. It is with trembling hands that I now put quill to paper. Much of my soul they destroyed, but my ability to write, they could not vanquish that. Not without severing my hands, but I would not have been able to labour night and day for them, toiling without nourishment or rest. Who are the faceless 'they' I talk of? They are evil incarnate, they are fear in its purest form. This I write in order that others may learn of them. They must be stopped. Who has the power to defeat them I cannot say.

My home was once a small village on the outskirts of Marienburg. They came in the dark of night, striking with the swiftness of a falcon, silent and in small numbers. They did not need many, such was their skill and stealth they were upon us before any alarm was raised. My only solace was that my wife was visiting relatives in the next village. From my bed they dragged me outside, I remember how my neighbour's child cried, his mother trying to comfort him, but the child sensed his mother's fear and his wailing did not cease. They tore the screaming child from his mother's arms and took him away. I remember the silence that followed and how haunting it felt. No one ever spoke of the child again and his mother was silent in her despair.

At knifepoint we were led to their dark vessel. A great mountain, blacker than night loomed before us. Tall spiked towers reached into the sky, obscuring the constellations. It was then that I knew that our gods had forsaken us. On a small boat we were carried to the nightmarish floating citadel. At times the calm sea would be broken by the gigantic ripples of some terrible beast beneath the surface. What horrors lurked in the waters where I had once swum I dared not guess. On reaching the fortress we were chained together, and so it was we were taken single file down into the depths of the Black Ark. Silent, save for the ominous rattle of our chains, we stepped down a steep spiral stairway. For what seemed like an eternity we marched into the bowels of hell. Occasionally a hideous scream from one of the passageways off the stairwell would chill my soul with a deep fear. It was the fear born of the knowledge that some time soon the despair I felt in my heart would join that chorus of pain.

Like cattle we were crammed into a dark chamber. On wooden racks we slept; there was no latrine, nor was there enough room for a man to stretch to his full length. For how long we were kept like this I cannot tell nor do I choose to guess. The filth that covered us soon developed into sores and before long disease was rampant. Our sleep was disturbed by the cries of those suffering from delirious fevers. The man chained next to me, a simple goatherd from our village, grew weaker with lack of sustenance. For many nights his body was wracked with a heavy fever before he was finally granted peace in death. By the time they finally unchained him from my side his corpse was bloated and maggots feasted on his putrid flesh. Others would occasionally join us, some of them races that I knew not from where they came. There was no conversation between us. I remember two of the foreigners were caught in conversation by a guard. He drew his wicked blade and sliced their tongues from their mouths. Both died a few hours later from choking on their own blood.

Slowly I succumbed to the nameless disease that crept upon us. In a delirium of fever I can vaguely remember being led from the chamber back up the stairway. How my legs were able to carry my emaciated body I cannot say. My first sight of the dark city of Har Ganeth was one tinged with the madness of my condition. Each of the tall towers was crowned with a hellish skull that tormented me in my delusion. Visions of our mortal future, they mocked me. Death was amongst us and my mind had little trouble conceiving that we had been transported to hell. Only three of the thirty slaves who had been taken from my village remained alive. We were separated into groups and sharp barbed spears prodded us towards our new masters who stood waiting at the end of the dock.

"Kehmor is my name, I am the slavemaster of Lord Ruerl and that is all you pitiful wretches need to know of me. Gone are the days when your lives were made complex by the choices that freedom allowed you. Your life will be simple now, obey me or die." I recall his words well, even though my mind was clouded by illness. As each of us passed him he branded our left chest with the mark of Ruerl. A black rune now scars the spot where I once perceived my heart to lie. Our new quarters were little better than those on the Ark. Cold stone replaced the wooden racks but we were still chained and crushed together. We were to work in the mines, digging the ores that would enable this race to forge more of their weapons, more power with which they could pillage and conquer. It was an endless cycle of despair. Night and day became concepts that existed only in my dreams. Soon I ceased to even dream. We were chained together by solid steel-spiked neck collars, more like beasts than men. If one of us tired from the solid work he would be whipped until his back was raw. If one of us should collapse from exhaustion the guards would sever his head from his body with great blades, rather than unlock his collar.

Even in our brief times of rest they would appear. Sometimes they would give us raw meat on a plate. Where it came from I dared not think, eating it with savage greed like some feral beast. Sometimes they would enter the cell and take one of us away. Of the poor soul's fates I cannot say. Screams of pain would usually follow such abductions. For how long I continued to slave in the mines I cannot estimate, but one morning I was led out of the cell by the guards. My mind raced with visions of the torments that I was about to suffer, but fate spared me any real anguish. I was taken to the forests where I was to cut down the mighty pines that covered the mountainside. Their girth is such that it would take ten men to link arms around even the smallest of these giant firs. For countless centuries these ancient trees had grown but, as is the wont of these dark masters, they were cut down in spiteful greed. We would be forced to work in the savage rain and biting snow with just torn rags for clothing. Though the fierce weather of Naggaroth nearly killed me, it was these same foul conditions that granted me freedom. On one wet cold morning I found an old dagger at the foot of one of the trees. Tempted as I was to slay my evil master I knew that swift retribution would follow. The damp mines and the rain had gradually caused my collar to rust. That night I used the dagger, which I had smuggled into my cell, to work loose my shackles. The next day as soon, as we reached the forest, I broke free and fled.

Up into the mountains I ran and, though my legs ached with exhaustion, I found strength in the knowledge that I was free. Behind me the beast-like hounds of my masters bayed. Through the icy streams I swam, to turn their keen nostrils from my scent. For many days they pursued me. A lone slave was of no great importance to them – they hunted me down for their own pleasures. Occasionally I would spy my former captors riding atop great monstrous lizards. The thought of being caught would send a shiver of pure fear through me. These beasts looked capable of tearing me apart as though I was a piece of parchment. High in the jagged dark mountains I hid, always heading west. I did not know to where, but my destination was anyplace away from the murderous attentions of those who sought to enslave me.

My captors called the mountain range the Spiteful Peaks. They were aptly named for they gave no nourishment to me. Neither beast nor plant survived in these accursed rocks. On the third day a monstrous shadow passed overhead. I do not know what manner of creature it was, but its head was that of a lion yet it flew with the wings of a great wyrm. In my past I would have thanked Sigmar that he made the beast blind to my presence but Sigmar had long since deserted me. That evening I spied tendrils of smoke rising into the sky. Cautiously I approached: if it were my hunters then I would face them and with my dagger take as many as I could to their graves. As I neared the encampment it was not the cold sharp tongue of the Druchii that met my ears. In the stranger's conversation I heard the unmistakable accents of Tilea and Estalia. Then my heart rose as I heard the familiar rough accent of a Middenlander. I dared not approach immediately, but instead sat for a while listening to their talk. Much time had passed since I last heard warm conversation but finally the lure of cooked meat bade me approach.

Now I sit here in those very same hills. Over the past months many others have flocked to our group. Rumours of a slave army have given heart to many and have lent them the will to escape and join us, but now they have also brought the enemy to us. We have amassed a small amount of equipment from raids into enemy encampments, but I would be loath to call us an army. We are ill-nourished and have only hatred of those who seek to enslave us as our weapon. Still, if we are to inspire any hope for others we know that we must go to war. As the most learned member of the group I have been chosen as their leader, yet I have no experience of war. I write this on the eve of battle with my former master Lord Ruerl. In our hearts we know we are defeated, yet should this letter manage to find its way into safe hands then know this. It is better to die fighting this cold, evil race than suffer the unthinking torment that they will surely inflict upon you. With this I leave to meet my fate on the field of battle, but know this, whatever may pass I will not be taken alive.

THE FOUNDING OF NAGGAROTH

as told by Furion of Clar Karond

I was old even when the world was still young, and thus it is I who writes of the long gone days, of millennia of hate, treachery and betrayal. I write to you, young Druchii, for I know the truth. I have stood among the ruins of Anlec and I have circled the world on my Black Ark, the Claw of Dominion. I will tell of the world as it was, for I have eaten the fruit of the Black Tree and, by the will of the Witch King, I have lived through ages even as my comrades have died. Thus I can tell you, Elf of true blood, of your past.

Though we have wandered far to this land, called the New World by the hairy barbarians, the usurper humans, we have not forgotten the spires of Anlec and our forests of pale grey trees. For this place was not always our home.

Your true home and mine lies far away from here, across the Sea of Chaos. Once Nagarythe was the greatest of Elven kingdoms. The beauty of our northern shores were famed throughout the world, and the folk of Nagarythe were known as the greatest warriors of all Elvenkind. There were also lesser Elven kingdoms, pale shadows of Nagarythe, insignificant in importance compared to our glory.

AENARION AND THE FIRST WAR AGAINST CHAOS

It was Aenarion the Defender, first Phoenix King, the ruler of Nagarythe, who waged a great war against the minions of the Four Powers in the immeasurably distant past. He wed Lady Morathi, and sired Malekith, the greatest of all Elves who has lived.

Aenarion fought and we, the folk of Nagarythe, fought beside him. After the First War against Chaos we stood victorious, and all of Ulthuan was in our debt.

Aenarion was slain in battle and, quite rightfully, his son Malekith requested the sceptre of Ulthuan for himself, for he was son of the King, born to rule, and the only Elf with a legal claim to the throne. But there were jealous lords, petty princes of lesser kingdoms who opposed noble Malekith with all their might. Rather than start a civil war, in his infinite wisdom Malekith suggested a vote for the throne. The ungrateful curs cast their votes and chose one of their own to take a task which was far beyond his capabilities. It was an outrageous insult to all of Nagarythe, and yet Malekith was first to acknowledge the rule of the lesser Elf, Bel Shanaar the Explorer, better known in our legends as the Pedlar-king.

Over the years Lord Malekith became ever more concerned. The enemies of the Elves had not disappeared, but Bel Shanaar did nothing to counter these threats. Long Malekith worked to strengthen the realm, but it was to no avail. Instead of facing the threat of the Dwarfs, who were bound to become our future enemies, Bel Shanaar cultivated peace agreements with the stunted folk.

Blinded by greed, he encouraged trade with the hairy ones when he should have prepared for war. The future would show how right Malekith was.

THE GLORY OF NAGARYTHE

While the rest of Ulthuan cavorted, the people of Nagarythe preserved our true heritage and, led by their lords, they trained in the skills of war and raised the art into new heights. The Cult of Pleasure produced the greatest songs of the age and Elves like Oeric and Aesabai made the most delicate and lifelike sculptures to grace the Gardens of Delight of Lady Morathi. Never has such beauty graced the known world, and not until we have claimed our rightful lands will it be recreated.

Flames of Asuryan. In the most tragic event of Druchii history, our lord was horribly scarred by the cursed flames, and his servants took him back to the north, to be nursed back to health by Lady Morathi and her priestesses.

But the princes of other kingdoms grew envious and coveted the riches of Nagarythe. They falsely accused Lady Morathi of treason and claimed that the Cult of Pleasure which she led planned to overthrow the king. Seeing no other way to save his people and his blood-kin from outright war, Lord Malekith called upon all his cunning and devised a plan to save the kingdom. He took control of the investigations into the innermost matters of the Cult, turning the agents of the Phoenix King against the petty princes who plotted the downfall of Nagarythe.

But in the end Malekith had no choice but to summon the Lords of Ulthuan to the Shrine of Asuryan to reveal the greatest traitor of all. Here Lord Malekith took Bel Shanaar to the Chamber of Days in the Shrine. Therein rests the Stone of Destiny which shows the events of the future in fiery letters, and here was revealed the eventual downfall of the Elves, thanks to the incompetence of Bel Shanaar.

Bel Shanaar, confronted with the magnitude of his failure, took poison as the traitor he was. Now Malekith prepared to save Elvenkind. But upon hearing of Bel Shanaar's death the petty princes drew their swords against Lord Malekith. Fools! They were like children facing a god. Long did Malekith try to make them see their folly, but finally he was forced to cut them down to defend his life.

To claim his rightful throne, Malekith donned the Feathered Cloak and stepped into the flames of Asuryan, for this is the way that the ruler of all Elven kingdoms is crowned to his office. But the envious princes had foreseen our Lord's rightful bid for the throne and cast vile curses upon the

FIRST WAR OF BETRAYAL

Meanwhile our enemies did not rest, but roused a rabble with their claims of the treachery of King Malekith. They placed a Caledorian thug known as Imrik on the throne and, after assuming the name Caledor, this ruthless tyrant started amassing armies to slay Malekith whom he greatly, and rightly, feared.

Soon armies of the pretender threatened our borders, and finally we were forced to draw arms against our misguided and envious brothers. The spearmen and archers of Cothique, the charioteers of Tiranoc and the cavalry of Ellyrion trampled the fields of Nagarythe underfoot.

But we knew great sorceries and no decadent Elven kingdom could match the glory of our arms. The lords of Chrace, Cothique, Ellyrion and Tiranoc could not withstand us, but fled howling before our weapons back to their pitiful abodes, there to brood, lick their wounds and plot petty revenge. Seeking to end the bloodshed once and for all we pursued them, cutting through the traitorous kingdoms of Tiranoc and Ellyrion like a fiery sword. From all over the Elven kingdoms those loyal to the rightful king Malekith gathered. From Saphery came the great mages who had cast their auguries and seen the just cause of our Lord Malekith. From Caledor came skilled priests who had grown disillusioned with the cripple god Vaul, and offered their services as weaponsmiths.

While war raged, King Malekith called his armourers to him and aided by Hotek, a wise and just noble who had once followed Vaul, they fashioned an unrivalled suit of armour. The king then mounted Baraug, his Dragon, and was made ready for battle, and the glorious armies of Nagarythe loyally followed behind him. Thus began the Longest War, and it will end when the last of our repugnant cousins is dragged screaming to the altar of Khaine.

Seven great battles Malekith fought, and he won them all, but Caledor the Traitor rallied numberless hordes of his kin, bound by lies and empty promises. By treachery and luck Caledor defeated King Malekith at the marches of Maldour, and with a fell blow slew great Baraug.

THE GREAT RITUAL

Now Malekith, determined to defend his kingdom, called the wisest sages amongst his followers, and prepared a great ritual. He planned to unravel the Great Vortex and summon the very legions of Chaos to earth, and bind them to his will. The priestesses of Lady Morathi, mightiest mages of the world, readily agreed. They would have succeeded had not a craven traitor, Urathion of Ullar, betrayed his lord and slipped away to inform the fops of Hoeth, hoping for reward of gold. For this deed he was slain by Kithan the Master Assassin, and to this day daemons rend his soul in the Void.

It has been claimed that the power of Chaos could have escaped from our control, but I was there and I knew our strength was sufficient. We were and are the masters of Chaos, and the howling powers of the Void are our servants. But the twisted scholars of Hoeth, alarmed by Urathion, disturbed the shades of the deceased resting in the Isle of Dead and their ghastly spells unleashed a terrible force to sink the lands of Nagarythe. A tidal wave, fully one thousand feet high, crashed upon our beautiful lands.

To save our people from this cataclysm, the wizards of King Malekith cast great spells and the palaces and fortresses of Nagarythe broke free and floated on the surface of waves and amongst the skies. Thus were created the Black Arks, and our folk survived, preserving our legacy. But our great and beautiful kingdom was drowned under the waves. We grieved the wrongs done to us and swore revenge.

We did not need great patience for a chance to exact our vengeance, for Caledor built a navy and dared to bring it against our mighty Black Arks and wave-dancing vessels for many years, until our spells brought a storm upon his fleet and separated his ships. Our glorious fleet, which ruled the waves then as it does now, descended upon him. Rather than face the rightful king and his justice, Caledor took the coward's way out and committed suicide, jumping into the sea in full armour. Thus passed Caledor the Traitor. It was a fitting end to an Elf who had wrought so much harm upon his rightful liege lord.

THE CONSTRUCTION OF SIX CITIES AND THE DWARF WARS

Without Caledor leading them, the cowards of Ulthuan had little courage to harry us further. Thus the war ended and we retreated to Naggaroth, named after the memory of our beautiful lands, and fortified our abodes. We scoured the lands, exterminated and enslaved the repulsive human barbarians who lived there, and prepared for the war that was to come.

Our masons built six great cities that were divided amongst the lords of our folk. Naggarond, the tower of Chill, was reserved for King Malekith. Ghrond was granted to the house of Kalanth and as the bastion of the Cult of Khaela Mensha Khaine, the bloody-handed god. Hag Graef, Karond Kar, Har Ganeth and Clar Karond, the port of our navy, were divided between the king's most loyal followers. It took us many long years to erect our towers and build our defences, and meanwhile our kin in Ulthuan found new enemies: the race of Dwarfs in the distant lands of the east.

Some have said that it was us Druchii who incensed the Ugly Folk against the effete princes of Ulthuan. But know now that these things are mere lies and worse than lies. The Dwarfs hardly needed an excuse to begin the war, and our misguided cousins were quick to start hostilities. Thus was Malekith's prediction proved correct, and the Dwarfs became the enemies of the Elf race.

For an entire age the armies of the pretender ruler of Ulthuan and the Dwarf kings slew each other, and how we laughed at the reports of their folly! It is a testimony of the weakness of Ulthuan that they failed to crush these upstarts swiftly and mercilessly. Finally Caledor the Second managed to disgrace our entire race by falling under the axe of the Dwarf King Gotrek Starbreaker in single combat. I spit on his memory!

THE WAR IN THE NORTH

Our auguries chose that time to unleash our armies upon Ulthuan once more. When we finally attacked, we drove the Elves of Ulthuan to the southern lands in an irresistible force. From the rubble rose the city of Tor Anlec once again, the blazing diamond in the shattered crown of Nagarythe. We, the true rulers of Ulthuan had returned. War raged across the isle and much which was rightfully ours was regained. For centuries our ancestral lands were ours to rule and govern and, despite the necessities of war, prosperity and unsoiled heritage flourished.

But then Tethlis the Butcher, the scourge of life, was elected to rule Ulthuan. He was a relentless enemy and succeeded in whipping the soft Elves of Ulthuan into something resembling a fighting force. With a huge army he besieged Anlec and when, after a long and bitter battle, the city fell he ordered all Druchii survivors to be slain, including all our families who had returned to live in the land of their forefathers. From that day on we vowed never to show mercy to our twisted kin. Thus the weaklings of Ulthuan brought a terror upon their heads.

The last bitter battle, the Battle of the Waves, was fought in the Blighted Isle, which we guarded against those who would desecrate the holy place of Khaine with their presence. Our armies fought valiantly but to no avail: we were too heavily outnumbered. The altar of Khaine, and the Promised Sceptre of our king which rests there was lost to our lesser brethren. One day it shall be ours again, and unnumbered will be the souls offered to him upon its ancient bloodstained stone. Ah, glorious Khaine, a feast shall be his!

THE AGE OF HATEFUL PEACE

In Ulthuan, Bel-Korhandis succeeded Tethlis to the throne, continuing the long masquerade of false kings. He displayed new depths of corruption, so low had his kind sunken. As we built our navy and sent our armies to consolidate our hold over the northlands, he emptied the coffers of Ulthuan to build a tower of colossal proportions to match his ego. Here he collected decadent works of 'art' and filled his court with sycophants and courtiers who eroded the last vestiges of the Elven spirit.

Thus our weakling kin studied poetry, dancing, gardening and other nonsense, and we watched gleefully how they ran down their armies and forgot the last of the noble military tradition of our past. Truly they had become less than nothing, and scarcely worthy of bearing the name of Elves, the First Speakers. But we, with our memories burnt into our minds by the heat of battle, had forgotten nothing of our knowledge, and our wisdom grew over the centuries of Hateful Peace.

During these years we built and planned. The warbands of Chaos worshippers had long harried our northern border, and thus King Malekith in his wisdom ordered the construction of a series of fortresses to guard our lands. From that day on the rampaging Chaos hordes were kept in check. Our Black Arks established colonies in the southern continent of Lustria and in the far lands of Cathay. We fought many wars against the Dragon Throne of Cathay, and our victorious armies brought back many wonders of the East to enrich our kingdom and fill the Witch King's treasuries.

Years flew by and centuries passed. Yet another new king rose in Ulthuan, even more decadent than Bel-Korhandis, and we seized our chance. Even if we would have been allowed to choose the next so-called Phoenix, we could have hardly found a more inept ruler than Aethis the Weakling, the poet-king of Saphery.

Aethis completely neglected the armed forces and the navy like the fool he was. With the guard of Ulthuan down, we struck secretly, silently, and yet with all the customary power of Druchii. The bravest of our kin, and most talented in intrigue and webs of politics, went secretly to Ulthuan, and over the years their influence spread. We eventually had agents even at the court of the Phoenix King. They spread rumours of the death of great Malekith, lulling the toads of Ulthuan into a false sense of security. In secret we controlled much of the Elven kingdoms, without our lazy, blinded former kin ever suspecting.

For long years our agents fought their shadow war, but finally the order of Swordmasters of Hoeth turned against us. This brotherhood of oppressors and murderers was a most bitter enemy to our cause, and many heroes lost their lives in public executions – though many wrong suspects died as well, I might add, for we had woven our web of deception with care and attention.

Finally the ringleader of our agents, Girathon the King's Councillor was unmasked. Threatened with torture, he decided to fight like a true Elf and slew the weakling Aethis. This plunged Ulthuan into chaos, and for this deed the name of Girathon shall be gloried forever in our legends.

THE DAY OF BLOOD AND RENEWED WAR

The next choice to the throne of Ulthuan was truly laughable: Morvael was another prancing, effete scholar. I fondly remember the day when he sent a punitive expedition to Naggaroth. This day is remembered as the Day of Blood, and it is ranked as the greatest of our victories. An entire fleet, an armada of hundreds of ships, sailed into our trap and was annihilated at the Sea of Chill. We left none alive, and took our revenge for the sack of Anlec.

With the navy of Ulthuan crippled, our long-prepared counter-offensive was unleashed, spearheaded by drugged and screaming human slave warriors. Once more we erected the towers of Anlec, and reconquered all our lands between the Isles and the Griffon Gate. These were the heady days of our glory. Victory after victory was ours, and countless numbers died on the altars of Khaine.

Desperate, the lords of Ulthuan sent all of their sons to war: potters, carpenters and dung-caked farmers. We slaughtered these lambs in their thousands. The only right decision Morvael made was to appoint Menethus of Caledor as his general. He actually gave us quite some sport. With a huge numerical superiority of peasants and merchants, he finally pushed us back. We sprang ambushes and fought a fighting withdrawal, for we were loath to give up our ancestral lands easily. For each Druchii life lost we took the souls of ten lackeys of Morvael. Finally, we were forced to abandon Anlec and cast the great Black Arks adrift once more. Satisfied with the destruction of the armies of Ulthuan we returned to Nagarythe, where already we were assembling our reserves. Upon hearing how many warriors he had lost, Morvael cast

himself to the flames of Asuryan. He was the third Phoenix King to take his own life. Ha! For five thousand years Malekith has ruled as the Witch King of Druchii. He has not given any thought to the grave, only to the restoration of our kingdom. Truly the blood of gods flows in his veins, compared to the weak water which bloats the rulers of Ulthuan.

THE NEW AGE AND OUR GLORIOUS FUTURE

For the next thousand years, we devoted our lives to increasing our influence over the world. Our Black Arks ventured far and wide. From distant Cathay to the coasts of the Old World, the human animals have learned to dread us, and the forges of Naggarond work day and night as the Human, Orc, Goblin and Dwarf slaves toil to fill the armouries of the Witch King. The libraries of Karond Kar are filled with sixty thousand books of sorcery. The black stone tablets of Naggarond were carved so the legacy of our past would be carried to the generations that are to come. In the distant lands of the east we routed the armies of Cathay and took one hundred thousand prisoners in a single day.

In the southern jungles of Lustria we discovered the last rotten fruits of the civilisation of the Old Ones. We slew their reptilian guardians and ransacked their ruined temples, bringing their golden glyph plaques to our cities. From these our sorceresses gleaned much magical lore unknown to our enemies. We now hold the knowledge of the great magics of the past which unleashed Chaos upon this world, and know how to bend the Four Great Powers to our will. Yes, we have become the ultimate masters of sorcery.

Our gold and tales of the riches of Elven kingdoms lured the savage Norse to harry the coasts of Ulthuan, weakening their navy and creating confusion. With our spells we ensorcelled the Dragons of Caledor so they would slumber deeply and could not be roused against us in war.

Just three hundred years ago, we made a pact with our old enemies, the lords of Chaos, and our combined armies took the Blighted Isle and lands of Nagarythe. The Plague Fleet and the Black Arks swept the seas clear of Ulthuan's navy.

Our lord Malekith himself returned to the soil of his rightful kingdom. With his leadership we won a score of great battles, and all the lands of Ulthuan save for Caledor, Saphery and the city of Lothern were under our dominion. But thanks to the incompetence of our Chaos allies and the twice-accursed brothers Tyrion and Teclis, the final battle was lost, though much of Ulthuan was devastated. We recalled our armies and the Witch King himself had to escape through the dark dimensions of the Void.

The current era is, to my mind, a time of consolidation and renewal. We have made great gains, and we have embraced this dusktime of the world with both hands. The next incursion of Chaos is near, and we shall ride the storm of Chaos and become like the gods themselves.

Now we are finally ready, our plans flawless, our armies unmatched, our hatred undimmed. Final victory is within our reach. But I grow weary of scribing, and I will rest. For tomorrow I will order my slaves to bring me my scimitar and the enchanted necklace made from the bones of my traitorous daughters, and I go to war once more. Serve the Witch King, young Druchii, and never forget your legacy.

The sharp edge of the blade traced a thin line of blood across the cheek of the captured human. Bound by his hands and feet with black silk cord to the bloodstained altar he struggled in vain. The Witch Elf lifted the dagger to her mouth and, with her delicate tongue, licked the tip of the knife. A small globule of blood trickled slowly down from the lips of the priestess and onto her pale breast. She thrust her head back and with both arms held high, raised the curved ceremonial dagger above her head. Uttering a violent scream that came from deep within, she plunged the dagger down. The Witch Elf screamed out again in an even higher pitch, her gasping shriek mixed with a ritual chant.

"Khaela Furdiekh Mensha Farmiekh Khaine!"

The cries of her captive added to the chorus, the two blending together perfectly in the rite of death. Breathing out deeply, she withdrew the blade, letting it slip from her moist, blood-soaked fingers to clatter onto the temple floor. With a speed that even the most agile human could never match, she jumped up onto the altar, her thin but muscular legs astride the dying man's chest. Arching her back in a sleek curve she slowly lowered her body until her face was inches from the wide-open eyes of her victim. Staring intensely into his motionless eyes for a brief moment, she leant down further, brushing her cheek against his. She pushed her deep red lips against his ear letting her long dark hair fall across his face. In a soft sultry whisper she spoke to him. As she spoke in the native tongue of her victim, her voice lost the sharp tones of the Druchii language, now her voice had changed into a soft purr of satisfied content.

"They say that your brain will continue to function for minutes after your heart has stopped. I can see the spark of life dying in your eyes."

Her wicked smile increased as she ran a finger through the blood dripping from his cut cheek.

"Know this then before you die. Your body will serve to pleasure me long after your soul fades. I will drink from your wounds and when my thirst is quenched I will bathe in your blood. Only when your body grows cold will I throw the empty husk of your mortal shell for the beasts to rip asunder."

She sat back up, squeezing her thighs tighter against the dead soldier. Her long, thin fingers delicately traced arcane runes in blood across his broad chest. Khaine would reward her well for this sacrifice and tonight she would revel in his gift of eternal beauty. She felt herself suffused by the joy of the moment, rapture filling her mind. It lasted only a few heartbeats though, and was soon replaced by the grim thought that Khaine was a capricious god and tomorrow it might be her that was beneath the sacrificial blade.

Lord Yeurl sat atop his Cold One and looked at the human army arrayed before him while absently stroking his fingers over the rough texture of his Orc hide saddle.

"Do you think they mean to fight us?" he asked, turning to his advisor, Khalek.

"I believe they do, my lord," Khalek replied smoothly, letting his gaze pass over the assembled army from the lands known to the humans as Bretonnia. "They have many cavalry, sire, and we are on an open field."

"Yes they do," Yeurl replied, stifling a yawn. "Bring out the slaves, Khalek."

"Sire?" the advisor's face wore his usual bland expression, but the tone of his voice caused the young Dark Elf lord to frown.

"Is there some problem with the slaves?" he asked quietly.

"No, my lord Yeurl," Khalek answered quickly. "I am merely curious as to what cunning ploy my lord has devised."

"Bring the slaves forth and you will see, my impatient counsellor," Yeurl told him with a sly smile.

The order was called out and soon the slaves, nearly five hundred of them, were being herded onto the field of battle, whipped along by the slavemasters.

"Let them go!" Yeurl called out, and the ropes binding the slaves together were cut. They milled about in a confused fashion. "Flee, you verminous filth!" screeched Yeurl in the crude human tongue, standing up in his stirrups and shooing them away. The slaves gave him a final bewildered look and then began to run towards the Bretonnian line.

"My Lord!" protested Khalek. "Think of your profits from this venture!"

"Khalek, old friend," Yeurl explained, as if talking to a stupid human, "my profits are worthless if I do not survive to benefit from them."

"Of course, my Lord," Khalek nodded slowly. "How short-sighted of me not to consider that."

Yeurl looked towards Saradain, the commander of the crossbowmen, and nodded once. The lithe Dark Elf raised his arm and, at the gesture, a hundred repeater crossbows were lifted to the firing position. Saradain's arm dropped and the air was filled with a cloud of black shafts that tore into the fleeing slaves. Salvo after salvo rapidly followed, felling even more of the escaping humans as they began to slow and stumble over their dead comrades. One particularly lucky or agile man was still running, and soon the cheers of the Bretonnian army resounded across the field, encouraging the fleeing man. Saradain looked to Yeurl, who shook his head once. With another gesture, he commanded his warriors to lower their weapons.

The roaring cheers of the Bretonnians were still rising, the escaped slave was now almost halfway across the field. With a nonchalant slowness, Yeurl reached down and unhooked his repeater crossbow from his saddle. Sighting along its length, he saw that a group of the Bretonnian commoners were riding out to fetch the bedraggled man now stumbling with exhaustion

towards them. Breathing slowly, Yeurl closed his eyes and pulled the trigger on the crossbow. The bolt flashed out across the grass of the meadow, but it was clear the shot would fall wide of its mark. As the bolt arced down it veered in flight, turning to its right. A moment later the magical dart was chasing down the slave, who glanced back over his shoulder and gave a scream a moment before the bolt took him square between the shoulder blades. The slave pitched forward and the cheers of the enemy soon became moans of dismay and angry shouts.

"Well, Khalek," Yeurl said smugly, waving an expressive hand to indicate the carnage just wrought. The bodies of the dead were piled in hummocks and mounds that littered the smooth expanse of grass. Already crows were descending to feast on the still warm bodies. Yeurl caught a faint glimmer of movement and noticed that two parties of his Shades, his best scouts from the craggy mountains of Naggaroth, were already taking up position amongst the dead. "You were saying something about cavalry and an open field?"

Khalek did not reply and hid his anger well, though the young lord still noted a hint of a frown. Yeurl held out his right hand, the fingers open. He sat there for a moment until a look of displeasure crossed his face.

"My lance," he snapped, turning to glare at the Dark Elf standing behind his mount, who hurried forward with the long, elegant weapon. He was new, and he wouldn't survive long if he didn't improve, thought Yeurl as his long fingers closed around the padded grip of the lance. Two ribbons, one of black, the other of ice blue, fluttered from its tip in the wind. Resting the lance in the ornate stirrup of his saddle, he turned to his left and spoke with the other knights.

"It seems these humans want to fight us!" he declared with a grin, causing his knights to erupt with a chorus of cheering. Kicking his wicked spurs into the flanks of the Cold One, he led the advance, his knights forming up around him, the infantry running alongside to his left and right, taking cover amongst the piles of slave corpses.

"I want their general's head!" snarled Yeurl as the fighting spirit took hold of him. His blood coursed through his veins, he could feel his heart beating in his chest like the thunder of a storm. He was panting with exertion and anticipation as the unit wheeled to square off against the unit of Bretonnians surrounding the largest enemy banner. Yeurl assumed his opponent would be here and smiled to himself. Another trophy would adorn the walls of his keep when he returned to Naggaroth,

"For Tor Anlec!" he bellowed, lowering his lance to full tilt. The humans were counter-charging, but the mounds of dead impeded their horses. The whinnying of horses and the snarling of the Cold Ones filled Yeurl's ears. The Dark Elf could see the enemy general, his armour gilded and polished, glaring in the midday sun. He sat upon a fine black steed, one which Yeurl swore could have been bred in Naggaroth, such was its fiery temper. In his hand he wielded an etched blade, probably blessed, thought Yeurl as he brought his lance point towards his foe. Their eyes locked, the human with his sword raised for a downward slash, his shield brought across his body to deflect Yeurl's lance.

The human's eyes flickered away momentarily as his mount stumbled on a dead slave, and Yeurl made his move, hauling the Cold One to the left, and swinging the lance across to his other side. The Bretonnian duke tried to pull his shield across but was too late, Yeurl's lance punched through the armour beneath his upraised sword arm, smashing the duke from his saddle. His Cold One leapt upon the black horse, its claws gouging into its chest in a spray of blood as its jaws closed on its throat. As Yeurl shrieked with joy, he looked about him. His knights were battling all around, a few had fallen but not as many as the enemy.

"Let your blades drink deep!" he cried out to his comrades, discarding his lance and drawing a longsword from its scabbard. A lance was thrust towards his face from out of the mêlée, but Yeurl easily swayed out of its path, severing its tip with a casual flick of his blade. His counter-attack crashed onto the shield of the human, almost unhorsing him. Through the narrow visor, Yeurl could see the hatred burning in his foe's eyes, and felt invigorated by it. Let their hatred flow, he told himself, for I know what true hatred is. Snarling an oath, he brought his sword around in a whistling arc, slashing beneath his opponent's raised shield at the last moment, the blade severing the knight's leg at the knee. Yeurl laughed into the sky as his opponent fell clumsily from his saddle with a clattering of armour.

The human knights tried to scatter and run, but the Cold Ones had encircled them and the few who were left were swiftly butchered. Gasping for breath, Yeurl pulled his helm free and gulped in the warm summer air. All around, the dead and dying Bretonnians littered the field amongst the corpses of the slain slaves. A fitting end for such beasts, Yeurl thought. To his right, he saw Saradain had surrounded the human peasants and many held their hands up in surrender. Shielding his eyes against the glaring sun, Yeurl could see there were several hundred who begged for mercy; some wounded, others simply fearing for their lives.

Yeurl was content as he dropped off his Cold One and searched amongst the dead knights for the general he had killed. He had more slaves to replace those he had been forced to kill and, as he hacked off the lifeless head of the Bretonnian duke, he felt the warm rays of the sun bathing his face. Today was a good day.

My Lord,

I have compiled on your instruction all the information that I can find concerning the forbidden practice of the worship of Khaine. Unfortunately Johann Holstrum, the first of the appointed Theogonists, destroyed nearly all of the records in a purge of flame. Whilst I command his diligence and wholehearted fervour to destroy the evil cult, I cannot help but feel that in our ignorance we have simply removed the body of the parasite whilst its head still works its way through our arteries to our heart.

Of the information I managed to recover I was alarmingly disturbed at the findings and would suggest an immediate council be appointed to deal with the threat.

Unlike the Chaos cults that more openly preach to the heathen masses, the worshippers of Khaine are far more secretive. From what little knowledge I possess on the subject and the manuscripts I have recovered, I can without doubt be certain that, even now in these enlightened times, there are those who worship Khaine the god of murder. Imperial records find that his worship can be traced back to the year 80 in the calendar of Sigmar, when agents of the Theogonist discovered the existence of a number of worshippers inside the town of Marienburg. They were of course burned at the stake, but not before torture revealed that the foundations of the cult were far deeper rooted than suspected. Many of the worshippers came from outlying farmsteads and villages who had come into contact with Elvenkind. It was at this point that I expanded my search to include Elven literary records, for all Elves, it would seem that Khaine is an integral part of their belief. For even those Elves who abhor his worship, Khaine is a necessary element to their way of life; without pain there can be no pleasure, without evil there can be no good. Such fundamental flaws in their beliefs would certainly explain their thirst for war against each other. The Elves from a province known as Nagarythe were devout worshippers of Khaine. Hardened by a constant struggle against the forces of Chaos that descended from the north, the worship of Khaine gifted these Elves with a necessary brutality. If I understand the context of their language it would seem that they were a dark and sombre race and revelled in self indulgence. It was only through the worship of Khaine that they became a more focused nation which ultimately led to civil war amongst their own kind. When the exiled Elves fled west from Nagarythe, the worship of Khaine flourished in their new homeland. Few other religions can withstand the bloodshed that accompanies the worship of this dark god. Those who oppose him in their new land which they named Naggaroth soon find themselves upon an altar doomed to be sacrificed in his name. The open worship of Khaine leads to war and depravity on a scale unsurpassed by any other following.

Now is the time to be vigilant, the time for action. Who can say how many have already been sacrificed in Khaine's name in our own great Empire? Who can tell how many of the murders that darken our streets each night are committed in his name? It is within the nature of those who worship Khaine to remain silent and breed sinister but should this vile worship ever take hold within the general populace then I fear the co... therefore call a meeting of the Council to discuss best how to deal with this threat.

Sigmar protect us

G... ...

This rite ...
before the ...
will furthe...
decades, giv...
look of innoce...

Ingredients

1qrt Fresh W...
optimum effe...
months of age...

2 Freshly pluck...

1 Eyeball of an 1...

The Right Hand of...

Sacred Oil extract...
unicorn.

Crush the beating heart...
simultaneously, letting...
that of the innocent chi...
over night in the Sacred ...
on the burning flames o...
Drop the flaming eyeb...
in a circular motion ...
holy man, recanting th...
times.

Best served warm.

Lock up your children, shut all windows tight.
The Witch Elves are hunting for victims tonight.
When old hags do knock at your door, you must hide,
Your death is the gift sought by Khaine's pretty brides.

Traditional nursery rhyme sung on Death
Night by Dark Elf Children

A letter from the Grand Theogonist to Karl Franz written shortly before the Council ordered all libraries and monasteries to destroy any literature pertaining to Khaine.

For you i Sla...
Upon your altar we sacrifice.
Blessed the blood shed by thy knife.
in Hatred i will find your path
in Murder i fulfil your task.

With heart in hand i call ...
To smite my foes down with thy fear.

The sun sank below the horizon, reflecting a myriad of colours on the surface of the sea. In the darkening twilight, on the cold, sandy beach, a warrior drew his sword. Silhouetted in a thick unearthly mist to his left he could make out the image of a shrine. That was why they were here; the treasure within the temple would decide which of the factions would control the fate of Ulthuan. The Elf relished the coming battle. He felt the cold biting and the combat would at the very least turn his attentions away from the sharp frost that gnawed throughout his entire body.

He knew it would be a bitter and bloody fight, and something deep within his consciousness told him he would not live to see the conclusion. Pushing such thoughts aside, he advanced forward with the rest of his regiment. How dare the arrogant Avelornians invade his land! Had not he and his kin struggled for many years against the invasion of Chaos? Many citizens of Nagarythe had died protecting the people of Ulthuan and their reward was betrayal. For that he would make them suffer. They were a proud, vain people and that was their weakness. A deep rage began to swell inside him. This was his enemy, they had always been so.

A young spearman, his features masked by the tall silver helm of his people, stepped from the mist to challenge him. His face was familiar; he had seen this Avelornian before. The warrior searched his memory for some scant recognition but none came. He easily parried a low thrust; he had seen the attack coming and had learned how to defend from such moves. He had parried that blow a thousand times now. Bringing his blade upward in a powerful arc, he already knew it would kill the young warrior. His sharp steel cut a deep gash in the white tunic of the Elf. A red stain spread across his chest as the Avelornian sank to his knees before being consumed by the mist that swirled at their feet. Another assailant stepped forward, his face too sparked some recollection in the warrior's eyes. Something deep within his consciousness told him that this warrior would trip and that this would be his undoing. Even as this thought passed through the Dark Elf's mind his challenger stumbled on a rock, falling to the ground. The warrior thrust his blade down into the prone Avelornian's unprotected back, killing him instantly.

In a brief respite the warrior looked about the battlefield. To his left another Dark Elf slew his opponent. This warrior's armour and family insignia were unfamiliar to him. How could that be? He knew the emblems of each of the noble lines of Nagarythe and this was not one of them.

What strange ally had joined them in the slaughter? He had no time to investigate further. A sword arced downwards – it would miss him by inches. It always missed. Again he recognised the features of his opponent; the scar on his cheek, the look of horror that would appear on his face when his armour was pierced. The warrior thrust out with his bloodied blade, his opponent's scale mail tearing open, allowing the sharp sword to slide through him with ease.

The Dark Elf waited for another opponent to appear through the mist, but none would come, there were no more for him to slay. A route to the shrine lay clear in front of him now. Inside it lay the sword of Khaine, forged by the Elf smith god Vaul, such was its power that he who wielded it could challenge the gods themselves. If he could reach it, he could deliver it to Lord Malekith, perhaps even he could use its power to stop this war. He would bring peace to Ulthuan, uniting the Elves together so once again they could rule supreme over the world.

He ran up the black marble steps, although he knew that he would never reach the top; here on the last step he would meet his fate, here he would die. Yet how? There were no warriors to stop him, no one to challenge him. Perhaps the emotion of battle had clouded his thoughts. A sharp sting struck him in his back and he remembered, an instant before seeing, the arrowhead which had burst out of his chest. The warrior collapsed to his knees, slowly feeling his life ebb away, as it had done a thousand times over. As suddenly as it had appeared his body dissipated into the mist.

One by one, each of the warriors fell, their bodies vanishing as they hit the ground. Generations of Elves were doomed forever to fight each other in an afterlife of war.

As the morning sun rose, the mists that shrouded the land cleared. The empty beach showed no signs that a battle had been fought the previous night. The sand dunes that covered the region were undisturbed by the marks of the skirmish, no carrion feasted on the flesh of the dead. Only the white bones of long-dead warriors rose from the windswept sands, destined to be reclaimed at some future time by the `shifting dunes. The small band of Shadow Warriors that guarded the temple slipped silently down from the crest of a tall dune. They had spotted a group of Druchii raiders making their way across the dune-filled plain and swiftly moved to intercept them. The next night, the spirits of yet more doomed warriors would swell the armies in the eternal struggle that was waged upon the Blighted Isle.

Kaleth Blackheart prodded his spear down through the gratings that kept the prisoners secure within the hold of the small ship. He could see the tall spiked towers of his homeland and was eager to refresh himself. He spat at one of the slaves,

"The sooner we get to the city the quicker I rid myself of your ugly company." He thrust the tip of his spear at the captive below him. The raiding party would be at the gates of Karond Kar within the hour, for Kaleth though it was not soon enough. The sun was setting and unless they picked up speed the group would not make it to the city harbour before nightfall. The journey had been a rough voyage already and Kaleth was eager to get off the small vessel. He much preferred the safety of travelling in the massive Black Arks. On this voyage alone they had twice been forced to evade the attentions of the High Elf patrol ships and as they had neared the Dyre Straits a many tentacled leviathan had surfaced, grasping a dozen crewmen from the deck of the ship and dragging them down to the dark depths of the ocean.

Still, the ship was nearing its destination and the once the precious cargo had been unloaded Kaleth doubted that he would have to make any similar voyages for many years to come. Slaves were a valuable commodity and any Dark Elf noble willing to fund a raiding

expedition could assure himself a great deal of wealth and prestige should it prove successful. His was a poor catch though, any slaves that had been worthy of capture had died in the defence of the village. The High Elf warriors had put up a stout defence, many of his Corsairs had fallen in the attack but against the black barbed bolts of their repeater crossbows they stood little chance. No living soul had been left within the village, his warriors had wanted to torch the dwellings, but Kaleth had refused them the pleasure. A deserted village would serve to haunt the dreams of any High Elves that came across it.

Those that had been left alive were either old and weak or very young. Still they were now captives and one way or another they would be put to good use by the Dark Elves. Those who were too frail to be put to work in the mines would find themselves on the sacrificial altars for the pleasure of Khaine's disciples. Even Kaleth had to suppress a shiver of fear as he thought of the fate awaiting those pitiful wretches. The Witch Elves had a unique talent for causing their victims to die an excruciatingly painful and agonising death.

The clouds that seemed to permanently hang over the city grew a menacing shade of black as the dark of night descended. Beneath these clouds Kaleth could make out the sacrificial pyres of the city. The hundreds of souls that perished each day within the city would be burned on those fires of an evening. Many thought the black cloud that shrouded the city were a result of these sacrificial flames and few ever questioned such belief. Kaleth could sense by the hurried shouts of the ship's captain that he too was dreading the imminent nightfall. The port of Karond Kar was surrounded by jagged rocks capable of tearing a hole in this small raiding ship as though it were soft flesh. But this was the least of the captain's fears. He was an experienced sailor and had navigated this route on many occasions. Karond Kar, the City of Despair as it was also known, was the first stop off point for the slave vessels returning from their raids on Ulthuan and the Old World. The strong winds that buffeted the tall spiked towers of the city carried with them an eerie howl. The Corsairs had told him the noise was the screams of dead spirits, the ghosts of prisoners who had died in anguish and had been buried far from their home soil. Hundreds of slaves from every continent were brought to this busy port to be sold to rich nobles and slavers.

The pyres served as beacons to guide the ships safely home, but nightfall brought with it a fresh and far greater menace. A shrill piercing shriek from high in the dark sky reminded Kaleth all too well of this threat. Karond Kar served as the home to the Harpies. During the daylight hours these creatures would roost upon the many tall towers that grew up from the city. Come dark, though, these deadly scavengers would fly above the city in great flocks seeking out weak and easy prey. A ship still out at sea would make all too much an

As the dread monsters ripped the young Elf apart, his screams merged with the chorus of waves crashing against nearby rocks and the savage cries of the Harpies. They were in a feeding frenzy, lashing out at the prey. Each snarled ferociously at each other as their razor sharp claws ripped great gashes across the chest of the prisoner. One by one they flew off carrying the severed limbs of their victim back to their roosts. As the last of them flapped its wings to head home the gnawed rope fell down to the ship deck landing in a pool of blood at the foot of the mast.

With the harpies stomachs full the ship and its crew would be granted safe passage now and Kaleth looked forward to the small but welcome purse he would receive for his catch. The captain barked out commands to steer the ship to the docks. Kaleth walked towards him waiting until he had issued his commands before engaging him, "That youth could have fetched me a tidy sum at the markets."

The captain turned to face him, "It was worth the cost to save my crewmen. You will of course be compensated for your loss as usual."

opportune target for Kaleth's liking. These creatures were said to have the ability to charm anyone with their enchanted songs and Kaleth for one did not relish the prospect of what they would do to him once they had him under their spell.

The captain too had heard the Harpy's high pitched scream and as more followed he began to bark orders to the crew. Kaleth the slave master did not need be told his duty. Unlocking the iron bars he ordered the nearest slave out of the hold. The slave climbed up the ladder slowly, his progress impeded by his shackles. Kaleth grabbed hold of the chain and dragged the slave to the upper deck.

He was a mere youth, Kaleth guessed his age to be less than one hundred. The defence of the village would almost certainly have been the first combat the boy would have seen. Still, if he was prepared to fight as a warrior then he should know the consequences. Quickly he caught a rope thrown to him from the rigging and hoisted the prisoner up the mast. The youth held his head high and remained silent, he would have made a fine warrior given a few decades more training.

Tying the other end of the rope to the foot of the mast, Kaleth ran to join the Corsairs who had drawn their swords and held them in a defensive position. Kaleth could not suppress smile of anticipation at the forthcoming spectacle. The wild flapping of leather wings caused him to stare up towards the bound victim. He could make out five or six of the creatures in the dim light. Grotesque wings and black, bestial scale-covered legs gave way to a voluptuous female body. Their wild hair blew in the wind, Kaleth was entranced by their strange feral beauty, and could quite easily see how legends told that they were the spirits of Witch Elves slain in battle. They hovered around the sacrificial offering for a brief moment before one of them screeched and attacked the youth, raking long talons at his unprotected body.

The great jaw snapped shut, ripping the High Elf in two. The dismembered torso fell to the ground as the Dragon arched its neck and searched for a new victim. The row of sharp spears thrust in vain at the hard scales that protected the tough dragon hide. With one mighty swing of his blade the Witch King beheaded three of his assailants. As their limp, lifeless bodies hit the floor the attack wavered. Even the brave High Elves knew that to fight such a powerful opponent was sheer folly. The Dragon let out a deafening roar and with that the spearmen broke. As they turned to escape, the great beast took in a deep breath, filling its massive lungs. With another loud bellow it released a cloud of thick noxious gas that enveloped the fleeing troops. In a matter of seconds each soldier was brought to his knees, gasping in vain for breath. Their lungs had been burnt by the corrosive acids in the Dragon's breath, each of them would suffocate to death in excruciating pain.

Malekith dug his heels into his stirrups. It was the signal that his mount was to take to the air. The beast stretched out its wings to their full span, casting a dark shadow over the bloodstained earth below. With just a couple of beats it had risen from the ground and, with an agility that was belied by the monster's size, it hovered over the carnage below. From his high vantage point the Dark Elf king could see that the battle was faring well. The charge of the Cold One Knights had broken the left flank of the High Elf line. Once through the solid formation, of spearmen the savage beasts had borne down upon the lines of archers with remarkable speed. His warriors had been victorious and, even as he looked around, were now gathering the captured High Elves into lines.

The ancient ruined palace of Anlec was now his again to rebuild and fortify. From here his forces could once more strike at the heart of Ulthuan.

He issued a command to the Dragon and it covered the distance between him and the ancient castle with remarkable speed. The creature landed upon the cracked marble stairs that had once led up to the throne room. From this palace Malekith and his mother Morathi had held court. He and his father alone understood the need for war. From this very land had his father not saved the fate of those Elves who now spat insults at his son? Malekith leapt down from his saddle and strode up the stairs towards the ruined entrance of the throne room. Though the roof had long since collapsed, the doors to the room were barred before him. Did the fools really believe that they could deny the rightful heir entry to his own throne room? With a single whispered word uttered from the mouth of Malekith, the ancient doors cracked before bursting open. A sorcerous wind tore through the small chamber creating whirlwinds of dust and debris.

Malekith found it strange that there had been no guard posted at the doors. Were the High Elves so vain in their own pride that they thought their army undefeatable?

"Come no further vile Druchii, this is not your realm to rule." The hidden challenger who spoke was calm and showed no sign of fear of the king of the Dark Elves.

"And who is this that dares tell me I may not rule over what is mine." The Witch King hissed out his reply, hatred boiling through his words. From behind the broken stone dais where the throne once sat, a single warrior stepped out. On his head he wore the ornate feathered helm of Yvresse, and the Witch King could sense a powerful magical field emanating from the sword the warrior held in his hand. In an instant Malekith knew who stood before him.

"Ah, the impetuous Eltharion. Has your vanity grown so great that you believe you can challenge me? Come fool meet your doom." As Malekith spoke his challenge Eltharion raised his sword in preparation for the combat. Malekith had little doubt he could slay the young warrior but he would not give Eltharion the satisfaction of honourable combat. Pointing his armoured gauntlet at the High Elf hero he uttered a single word. In an instant, Eltharion felt a darkness surround him, he clutched at his throat unable to breathe. His entire body coursed with pain, as though his blood had been turned to molten lead, tears of blood poured from his eyes and he fell to his knees in agony, his Fangsword slipping from his grasp.

The Witch King let out a malicious laugh. "You pitiful wretch, had you led your valiant men on the battlefield instead of cowering inside this palace then you may have stood a chance of defeating me. Know this before you die, none tread on my land without my word. Those who dare defy me suffer death." The Witch King stepped over to where Eltharion lay and, with a strength disguised by his thin, armour bound body, he picked up the High Elf by his neck and dragged him to the open doors. Over a hundred High Elves knelt in a long line, their hands tied behind their backs and their necks exposed. Over each of them stood one of Malekith's elite Executioners holding their terrible blades high in readiness.

"How fitting that the warden of Yvresse will be the first to acknowledge my succession to the throne of Ulthuan. For your loyalty I will spare the lives of your men; they are but misguided fools and under my rule they will learn the error of their ways."

Eltharion's pain multiplied tenfold with the knowledge that he had the lives of his men in his hands. But for his pride he could perhaps save those soldiers who had fought with him so valiantly on the shores of Naggaroth. He knew though that he could never bow to Malekith, his men would not wish it so either. With his last strength he raised his head in defiance.

"You are but a Prince of Darkness." As the words passed his lips his body sagged and fell into unconsciousness in the grasp of Malekith. In a dark rage the Dark Elf lord picked up the body of the noble hero, holding it over his head before casting him down the stairs.

"Have my most skilled torturers see that his spirit is broken and his body becomes little more than an empty husk," he ordered one of his commanders.

"What information would you have us extract from this sorrowful excuse for an Elf my Lord?" The commander bowed.

"There is nothing that this one can tell me. Once they have had their pleasure, have what is left of the noble Elf sent back to Lothern. It will be a warning of the fate of any who dare stand between me and what is rightfully mine." Malekith's eyes betrayed no sign of emotion, frozen in a deadly stare of contempt at the wounded Eltharion.

"And what of the prisoners?" the commander enquired.

"Kill them. Kill them all." His order was met by the dull thud of Elven heads as they were brutally separated from their torsos. As he walked back into the throne room and sat on the cold stone dais a smile passed his lips. Such slaughter would be the fate of any who defied him. The weak would die in order that the strong prevail.

Dark Power

Inside the dark chamber, the flickering light of a dozen candles illuminated the exotic and macabre ornaments that filled the sweet smelling room. The sorceress stood over a small boiling cauldron adding the last few ingredients into the black pot. As she sprinkled in a fine powder from her long delicate fingers it sparked into a dark blue flame. The potion was nearing completion and any mistake in the ritual preparation could now prove fatal. In a deep resonant voice she made the final incantation, the words spilling from her lips. It was as though the words had a life of their own; with each new one the air around the sorceress grew heavier. This was an old tongue, and the ancient words had the ability to destroy the very essence of life itself.

Morathi felt the magical power which she was summoning growing in strength. It was probing her mind searching for a path through which it could escape. The energies carried on growing and Morathi could feel her mind begin to surge. Visions of distant lands, the past and the future, formed before her. Should she choose, she could visit any of these worlds and travel through the corridors of this strange dimension. Quickly clearing her thoughts she focused upon releasing the spell. A dark aura grew and she could feel her long hair writhing and snaking with a life of its own as the magical essence was absorbed into her entire body. Pointing her finger at the cauldron, sparks of energy flashed about her. With the command of a single word, the magical energy was released and a bolt of black light burst from her hand into the bubbling liquid.

Morathi turned away from the cauldron, letting her body relax. Such concentration drained her of great amounts of strength. The Dark Powers had almost overcome her and lured her away from the real world. Had she chosen to travel down the paths open before her without the correct preparation, even she, the most powerful sorceress in the world, would have been easy prey to the daemons and dark creatures which stalked that realm. Morathi lay down on a luxurious four poster bed, collapsing upon the silk covers which enveloped her body. Against the black cloth her curved sleek figure was a contrasting white in colour. Her skin was smooth and almost like marble, upon her body there were no wrinkles of age.

There was still much work to be done before the potion was complete; she would have to carefully distil it into her small phials and even this simple task had its own dangers. Dealing with any form of magic was always a complex affair, but Morathi was well practised in such arts. As one of the oldest mortals to still walk the world, she had by now acquired a great deal of skill in the dark arts. For now though Morathi was content to rest on her bed as practising with such power always tired her and she felt in need of rest.

"I trust I'm not disturbing you." A voice came from her doorway, Morathi turned to face the uninvited visitor. There was but one person who would have the tenacity to enter her chamber without warning, her son Malekith.

"The Hag Queen has called council at the feast of Khaine, she has proof that the cult of Slaanesh has once again been active. She specifically requested you attend." Her son spoke as though he were some simple messenger rather than the king of his realm. Morathi smiled. He had learnt to use tact well, his voice betrayed no emotion.

Malekith approached the bed and sat down on the edge, Morathi sat upright, her silk robes revealing a sleek and ageless body beneath them. His armour was still coated with the blood of those slain in a recent battle. He removed his helmet and a long mane of silver white hair fell about his shoulders. His scarred face brought a fleeting stab of pain to Morathi. Even four thousand years after her son had been terribly marked, the anguish she felt when reminded of that fateful day had not diminished, she knew it never would.

"Ah Hellebron! Will she never learn that it is only through my will that her petty coven of hags still practice their primal arts? I could crush her with a single word. In truth they are my creatures; I do not serve the Witch Elves, they serve me." Morathi let out a small contemptuous laugh.

"Then do I assume you will not be attending the feast, mother?" Malekith's tone was still colourless, if he had an opinion on whether she should attend or not he was not freely giving such information away. Morathi was pleased her son was learning so much about the subtlety of politics and the importance of controlling his speech. He had yet to learn fully the extent to which his tone, speech, and indeed silence, could be read by his opponents and used against him.

"Malekith, I am impressed by your reserve, but you still have much to learn. I am bound to attend but it is not because Hellebron so commands. Should I choose I would have her killed tonight, but in doing so I would not gain. In fact my power would be weakened."

Malekith turned an attentive head towards his mother. Though he despised her for reminding him of his weakness she was right. His mother had a wisdom he could gain from. When this purpose was no longer of value to him he would punish her for her contemptuous attitude towards him. Until that day, though, he was content to learn from her, to suckle from her knowledge.

Morathi raised her hand, tenderly stroking her son's face as she continued.

"Hellebron's power over me is but one of the many lies that perpetuate her existence. It is one of the strengths of our culture, my son, that we do not readily embrace the truth. Each of the noble houses is built on the foundations of a lie. They believe that they have earned their power, and it is theirs to command. Ours is the only power in this kingdom, all else is but an illusion of grandeur. The truth behind such lies, my dearest Malekith, is that their power is little more than a gift to them from you." Morathi stroked her son's hair; she knew this always had a relaxing effect on him. "It is also a gift which we can take back at will." Malekith smiled at his mother's words; she had a way of bringing clarity to him.

"I attend the feast to perpetuate the lie, my son. Hellebron believes that she rules the temples. She truly believes that through her devotion the temple of Khaine is the sole religion of our people. In doing so she underestimates how deep rooted the worship of Slaanesh and his dark arts reach, and thus my sorceresses gain in power, unseen by the Witch Elves. Lies are power. They have the ability to change history. And history is built upon the lies of the victor."

Morathi laid back upon the bed and motioned for Malekith to join her.

"Come my son you must be tired after your little battle, lie with me and tell me how bravely you fought."

The chaotic nature from which Dark Magic draws much of its power attracts many malevolent spirits and dark sprites. They feed off the mysterious energies that are released and as a result can often be found hiding in the shadows around Sorceresses or other creatures of a magical nature. They are petty thieves, stealing away any small objects that take their fancy, but perhaps their most sinister act is the kidnapping of young babies. Nobody knows to what purpose they will occasionally steal away a child, but many a mother has woken to find her newborn babe vanished from the safety of its crib.

THE PATH OF SLAUGHTER
Arms and Armour of Dark Elf Nobility

1 Main figure – Lord Yeurl of Clar Karond. Cold One Knight arrayed in full harness of war; double swords a sign of noble birth; trophy head bound in flesh thorns a symbol of taking the soul as well as the life of the victim. The knight does not arm himself but is arrayed by two squires in a ritual sequence. The leg harness **(a)** is strapped on first and attached at the top to an underbelt, then the rere brace (upper arm armour) is laced in position. The knight's chest is then anointed with the symbol of Khaine in purified blood. A long, flowing robe known as a *khaitan* is then worn. The *khaitan* is often made from rich silk patterned with spells and charms. This robe is a Dark Elf symbol of war, and is worn by knights as a sign of martial status and prowess when not armoured.

2 Over the tunic, a padded aketon with mail sleeves and a long mail skirt is worn **(a)**. Called a *dalakoi* (lit. strength against death), the mail is lined with soft leather such as human or doeskin. This helps hold the mail in place. Back and breast plate **(b)** are then laced over the upper torso, sometimes these are one piece or also laminate strips for more flexibility. A short gorget **(c)** is then added. The pauldrons, or shoulder guards, appear to be more aesthetic than functional **(d)**; they are laced directly to the breastplate through the gorget. Occasionally they are one piece but normally are made from two or three connected plates; the laces are often left visible at the front, and are decorated with flesh hooks at the ends.

Long gloves with armoured hands are laced tightly to the forearm, and over these are fitted vambraces **(e)**. These appear to be one piece and held in place purely by the spring of the metal. They are often adorned with fighting spines – razor sharp blades which can trap and hold enemy blades as well as being weapons in their own right.

3 The helmet is a composite of separate parts. The main skull **(a)** follows a typical Dark Elf shape. The visor **(b)** is laced onto rings on the helmet (note the mail collar worn under the gorget), although often this is left off in battle to allow for maximum visibility in combat. The bevor **(c)** is laced directly and rigidly to the breastplate and makes a very effective guard for the vulnerable neck area.

4 Daggers and swords are slung on narrow crossbelts **(a)**. The number of weapons a knight carries is a symbol of his status at the Witch King's court, with two blades being the most common. Shields **(b)** vary enormously in shape, though all seem to have a recurved tip at the base that can be used as an offensive weapon. Lance tips **(c)** vary in shape and usually a long ribbon or pennant flutters beneath the tip. Runic script is often embroidered onto a knight's pennant, proclaiming their dedication to Malekith, their great deeds in his service and the noble history of their forefathers.

Also shown are two archaic weapons, only rarely seen in battle now, which are mostly used for ritual combat and duelling between the nobility. The shorter is known as a *ghlaith* **(d)**, which means spineblade, and is used for a paralysing blow to the lower back or limbs. The longer blade is called a soultaker **(e)**, *lakelui* in the *Druchii* tongue, and is used to dispatch the foe once they have been rendered defenceless. In such duels, failure to properly immobilise the foe before death will earn the displeasure of the audience and quite often leads to summary execution of the knight.

5 Flesh hooks – a selection of. Each is shaped as a *Druchii* rune, and the place and manner in which they are hung can tell a lot about a knight's allegiances, battle honours and family. With the flesh hooks are also hung janglers, known as *keikalla* or 'spirit bells', which serve a two-fold purpose. Firstly, the *Druchii* believe they ward away the most malicious of the magical spirits and entities that inhabit barren Naggaroth. Secondly, they serve to announce the presence of the knight, for unlike an Assassin or Shade, a knight rides proudly to battle in full view of his foes.

3a

2d

4c

3b

4e

2c

3c

a

4d

2b

2e

a

4a

5

4b

The howling of alarm horns woke Delekth from his slumber. As well as his own tower's alarm, he could make out at least three separate horns sounding out in the distance. He did not feel well rested; his sleep had been disturbed with terrible visions of dark and monstrous creatures. There were many Druchii who went insane due to the terrible nightmares which those who guarded the northern lands of Naggaroth would suffer. It was not uncommon for a warrior to throw himself from one of the tall towers which were dispersed at regular intervals across the land. Others would murder their fellow guards before taking their own lives. A sneer crossed over the sharp, cold face of Delekth at the thought; those warriors were weak, they deserved to die.

Delekth hastily put on his chainmail and grabbed his crossbow before running up the steep narrow spiral stairway. He reached his designated spy hole and looked out to see what danger approached. Looking out to the east he could see that a dank mist had already enveloped the neighbouring tower. An uneasy feeling crept over him, causing his stomach muscles to tighten. He had never seen a mist so dense or that rose so high before.

Thick tendrils of the eerie fog reached up to his portal, like writhing tentacles they seeped through as though they were trying to grab him. Peering down into the grey swirling cloud he spied movement. Something was rapidly ascending the open stairway that surrounded the tall pinnacle.

The Watchtowers reached hundreds of feet up into the sky, long thin bastions of rock atop of which was built a small stronghold. They had been constructed as the first line of defence against the incursions of Chaos that would sporadically sweep down from the Northern Wastes.

He rammed a cartridge of bolts home into his repeater crossbow and readied his aim towards the stairs. Whatever was climbing the tower was doing so quickly and he knew it would be upon them soon. Delekth heard the sound of guards firing their weapons from the level below, followed shortly afterwards by the unmistakable clatter of battle being met. Then he saw the first of his attackers as it scrambled up onto the tower platform. It was huge: monstrous horns were silhouetted throughout the mist and in its hands it wielded a massive sword. Behind it came another, then more.

Delekth did not hesitate, he fired a salvo of bolts into the monsters. The first fell, tumbling off the stairs but more swiftly took its place. The sound of hundreds of bolts whistling from their crossbows filled the corridor but still the creatures came at them. For each one that fell another two seemed to spring from the fog. From the level above, Delekth could hear the sound of a reaper bolt thrower. Its massive missiles shrieked as they sailed into the mist, followed by a dull thud as they struck home. There were too many of these creatures for the crew of the machine to miss. For a short while, Delekth could see that they were winning. The Daemons were not managing to close in on their position before being mowed down by the intense amount of missile fire. Then the lord of this horde appeared.

First he heard a monstrous roar that pierced even his cold heart with fear, then he spied the source of the sound. It swooped down from the sky, a massive creature towering over even the tall Daemons which swarmed up the tower. Its two monstrous wings were open wide, slowing the being's descent as it landed at the top of the stairwell. In its hand a huge flaming whip lit up the darkness of the mist revealing even more of the smaller Daemons. With renewed ferocity the dread host charged at the fortress. The speed of the assault surprised Delekth and he was glad to hear the order to retreat.

Springing up a stairway behind him, he heard the metallic groan of the portcullis buckling. With a deafening crash it broke and the Daemon horde poured into the tower. Behind him came the screams of those who were not fast enough to escape.

Reaching the top of the stairs, his heart dropped as he saw the guards closing it. Cursing their souls to Khaine, he looked for another avenue of escape; a few steps back he had passed a door leading into a store room. Charging through the small doorway he turned and bolted the thick wooden timbers shut. Quickly surveying his surroundings he realised that there was no escape from this small room, only the four solid stone walls and a bolted door in front of him. From outside he could hear the Daemons' claws as they raked on the stone stairway, and from a gap under the door he spied their menacing shadows as they passed by his hiding place. Delekth's heart beat fast as he waited for the Daemons to burst through the door, but none came. He heard the screams of those on the level above as the foul minions of Chaos broke through the upper defences, followed by a period of eerie silence.

As Delekth sat at the rear corner of the small room his mind raced. The Daemon host intent on killing those on the upper level must have missed him. How long had passed? Had the Daemons left? His mind twisted with a thousand unanswered questions.

Then movement from under the small gap at the base of the door broke his confused train of thought. As he watched, a tendril of mist crept into the room. Glowing luminescent in the darkness, it cast terrifying shadows on the walls. Backing himself into the far corner of the room Delekth drew his dagger to stab at the snakelike mist that seemed to be reaching out towards him, flooding into the enclosed room from under the door.

***

Lord Dranack dismounted from his Black Dragon. As commander of the northern wasteland it was his duty to investigate any incursions into Dark Elf territory.

"Report." He turned to address the Dark Elf guard who sprinted to meet him.

"Two of the towers were taken Lord," the guard replied, trying to catch his breath. "The mists have retreated now and our scouts have been able to enter them." The guard stood to attention as he addressed his master.

"What of the survivors?" the Druchii Lord coldly asked.

"None, my Lord." The guard replied, "Both towers were completely deserted save for the body of a single guardsman which we found locked within a storeroom. It would appear that he took his own life rather than face the Daemons."

The Dragon Lord sneered in contempt, "He was weak, he deserved to die."

The Underworld Sea is a vast labyrinth of tunnels and caverns that honeycomb the land beneath the Black Spine Mountains. Their chance discovery by the Dark Lord of Hag Graef meant that the raiding fleets of the Dark Elves now had the freedom of the oceans. Where once the superior naval capabilities of the High Elf fleet had confined the Dark Elves, now they were free to strike anywhere at will.

The tunnels are fraught with peril and, even on the main causeways, hundreds of strange and terrible monsters lurk. Tales tell of a fearsome race of creatures who prey upon the raiders but such legends are dismissed by the Dark Elf nobility as the ramblings of weak-minded fools.

RAIDERS OF NAGGAROTH

The lives of the Dark Elves are sustained by death and misery – the death and misery of the countless thousands of slaves that labour under the lashes of the slavemasters. The Dark Elf fleet sails across the world to loot the settlements of the other races, stealing what treasure and livestock they can find and imprisoning the inhabitants to be taken back to Naggaroth.

The bulk of such a raiding force is made up of Corsairs from the ships and Black Arks, who are led to suitable targets by a scouting force of Dark Riders and Shades. Occasionally the captain of a Corsair force will employ the services of sell-swords and cut throats who know the local area and are eminently disposable should his force run into any kind of opposing army.

On this and the next page are two special army list variants and a scenario that allow you to recreate a Dark Elf slaving expedition. It pits the raiders of a Dark Elf fleet against the defenders of an isolated settlement near to the coast. The scenario is a good starting point for a campaign involving Dark Elves, and you may want to use the Raiding army variant in subsequent battles.

THE RAIDING ARMY

The following modifications are made to the Dark Elf army list for the raiding force:

CHARACTERS

The Noble or Highborn leading the army is Captain of the ship and must be given a Sea Dragon cloak as a mark of his status. No Sorceresses are allowed.

CORE UNITS

Corsairs; Dark Riders

SPECIAL UNITS

Reaper Bolt Throwers, 0-1 Shades

RARE UNITS

Dogs of War

THE GARRISON ARMY

A standing garrison of soldiers will usually contain less noted individuals and officers, and has access to less specialist troops. For these reasons, the following modifications apply to the defending force.

The army contains one less character than it is normally allowed for its size. It may have a maximum of one Hero level Wizard.

The army must contain one more Core unit than the normal minimum for its size.

THE RAID

Overview: In this scenario the attackers must try to loot as much as possible and capture prisoners.

Armies: Both armies are chosen using the Warhammer army lists to an agreed points value, using the modifications given above.

Battlefield: An area roughly 24" square at the centre of the battlefield represents the settlement under attack, consisting of six or seven buildings, while scattered woods and the odd farm building may be used to break up the rest of the table.

DEPLOYMENT

Nominate one table edge as 'north'. The Dark Elf player writes down which table edge each of his units is going to attack from (north, south, east or west).

The Garrison force is set up anywhere within the settlement. Defending Scouts may be deployed anywhere on the table at least 10" from any table edge.

The Dark Elf player may deploy any Shades up to 10" in from the table edge they are assigned to, and at least 10" from any enemy.

Other Dark Elf units move onto the table from their nominated table edge on the first turn, as if they had just pursued an enemy off the table (see page 76 of the Warhammer rulebook).

Who goes first? The Dark Elves go first.

Length of game: The game lasts for 8 turns or until one player concedes defeat.

Special Rules: To enable units to fight inside the town, any infantry unit may use a Reform move to split into skirmish formation. It takes another Reform move to assume normal formation again. Units which are normally skirmishers may not assume regular formation and defending units may start the battle in skirmish formation.

Victory Conditions: The Dark Elf player scores Pillage points in two ways.

Looting buildings: Each building can be looted once by a Dark Elf unit entering it. This scores 2D6 Pillage points, rolled as soon as the unit enters the building. A unit may only loot one building per turn.

Prisoners: Any time an enemy unit is wiped out by a pursuing Dark Elf unit, roll a dice. On a roll of a 1 they are killed in the rout. On a 2 or more the unit is captured and scores the Dark Elf player a Pillage point for every model it contained when destroyed. Captured Heroes score 5 points each and captured Lords score 10 points each.

To see how well the Dark Elves have done, follow this procedure.

Divide the points value of the Dark Elf army by fifty.

Deduct this number from the total Pillage points scored and look up the result on the following chart:

Score	Result
-30 or less	Massacre to the Garrison
-20 to -29	Solid Victory to the Garrison
-10 to -19	Minor Victory to the Garrison
-9 to 9	Draw
10 to 19	Minor Victory to the Raiders
20 to 29	Solid Victory to the Raiders
30+	Massacre to the Raiders

Example: A 2,000 points Dark Elf army scores 65 Pillage points. Deducting 40 from this gives a result of 25, which is a Major Victory to the Dark Elves.

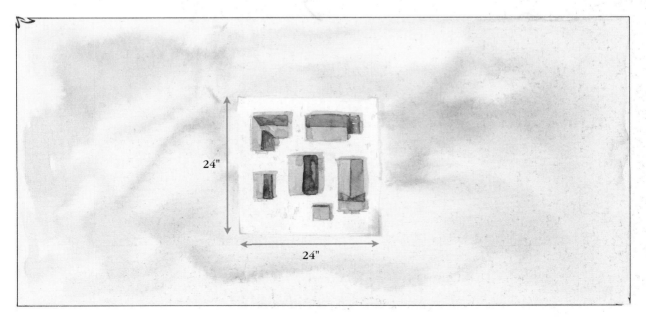

Lords	M	WS	BS	S	T	W	I	A	Ld	Special Rules
Highborn	5	7	6	4	3	3	8	4	10	*Hate* High Elves
High Sorceress	5	4	4	3	3	3	5	1	9	*Hate* High Elves; Sect Enmity
Heroes	**M**	**WS**	**BS**	**S**	**T**	**W**	**I**	**A**	**Ld**	**Special Rules**
Noble	5	6	6	4	3	2	7	3	9	*Hate* High Elves
Sorceress	5	4	4	3	3	2	5	1	8	*Hate* High Elves; Sect Enmity
Beastmaster	5	4	4	3	3	2	6	2	8	*Hate* High Elves; Beastmaster
Assassin	6	9	9	4	3	2	10	3	10	*Hate* High Elves; Hidden; Leadership
Core units	**M**	**WS**	**BS**	**S**	**T**	**W**	**I**	**A**	**Ld**	**Special Rules**
Warrior	5	4	4	3	3	1	5	1	8	*Hate* High Elves
Lordling	5	4	4	3	3	1	5	2	8	*Hate* High Elves
Corsair	5	4	4	3	3	1	5	1	8	*Hate* High Elves
Reaver	5	4	4	3	3	1	5	2	8	*Hate* High Elves
Dark Rider	5	4	4	3	3	1	5	1	8	*Hate* High Elves; Fast Cavalry
Herald	5	4	5	3	3	1	5	1	8	*Hate* High Elves; Fast Cavalry
Special units	**M**	**WS**	**BS**	**S**	**T**	**W**	**I**	**A**	**Ld**	**Special Rules**
Shade	5	4	4	3	3	1	5	1	8	*Hate* High Elves; Scouts; Skirmishers
Bloodshade	5	4	5	3	3	1	5	1	8	*Hate* High Elves; Scouts; Skirmishers
Witch Elf	5	5	4	3	3	1	6	1	8	*Hate* High Elves; Poisoned attacks; *Frenzy*; Devotees of Khaine
Hag	5	5	4	3	3	1	6	2	8	*Hate* High Elves; Poisoned attacks; *Frenzy*; Devotees of Khaine
Cold One Chariot	–	–	–	5	5	4	–	–	–	Chariot
Cold One Knight	5	5	4	3	3	1	5	1	8	*Hate* High Elves
Dread Knight	5	5	4	3	3	1	5	2	8	*Hate* High Elves
Executioner	5	5	4	3	3	1	5	1	8	*Hate* High Elves; Killing Blow
Draich-master	5	5	4	3	3	1	5	2	8	Hate High Elves; Killing Blow
Harpies	4	3	3	3	3	1	4	1	6	Flying Unit; Beasts
Rare units	**M**	**WS**	**BS**	**S**	**T**	**W**	**I**	**A**	**Ld**	**Special Rules**
War Hydra	6	4	0	5	5	6	2	5	6	Breathe Fire; *Terror*; Controlled; Large Target; Scaly Skin
Apprentice	5	4	4	3	3	1	5	1	8	*Hate* High Elves
Black Guard	5	5	4	3	3	1	6	1	9	*Hatred*; Stubborn
Master	5	5	4	3	3	1	6	2	9	*Hatred*; Stubborn
Reaper Bolt Thrower	–	–	–	–	7	3	–	–·	–	–
Beasts	**M**	**WS**	**BS**	**S**	**T**	**W**	**I**	**A**	**Ld**	**Special Rules**
Black Dragon	6	6	0	6	6	6	3	5	8	*Fly*; Cause *Terror*; Large Target; Scaly Skin; Noxious Breath
Manticore	6	5	0	5	5	4	5	4	5	*Fly*; Cause *Terror*; Large Target
Dark Pegasus	8	3	0	4	4	3	4	2	6	*Fly*; Impale
Dark Steed	9	3	0	3	3	1	4	1	5	–
Cold One	7	3	0	4	4	1	3	1	3	Scaly Skin; *Stupidity*; Cause *fear*

DARK MAGIC

CHILLWIND   5+
Magic missile; range 24"; D6 Strength 3 hits. Units taking casualties may not shoot in the next Shooting phase.

DOOMBOLT   6+
Magic missile; range 18"; D6 Strength 5 hits.

WORD OF PAIN   8+
Remains in Play
Range 24"; line of sight required. Models in affected unit reduce WS & BS to 1.

SOUL STEALER   9+
Range 6". All models in affected unit take Strength 3 hit. Sorceress gains +1 Wound for each unsaved wound caused, to a maximum of double her starting Wounds.

DOMINION   10+
Range 12". In the following enemy turn, Sorceress chooses: target unit may not move; target unit may not shoot; or unit may not cast Magic.

BLACK HORROR   12+
Centre 5" template within 18" and in line of sight. Models under template are wounded with no armour save on D6 roll over their Strength (6 always wounds). Unit suffering any wounds must take a Panic test.

> "We are the most civilised race in the world. We have more exquisite ways to kill than any other."
> *Lord Vraneth the Cruel, master of Har Ganeth*